DIVORCE HANDBOOK
FOR CALIFORNIA

DIVORCE HANDBOOK FOR CALIFORNIA

FIFTH EDITION

HOW TO DISSOLVE YOUR MARRIAGE WITHOUT DISASTER

Judge James W. Stewart

Impact Publishers,® Inc.

ATASCADERO, CALIFORNIA

ATTENTION ORGANIZATIONS AND CORPORATIONS:
This book is available at quantity discounts on bulk purchases for educational, business, or sales promotional use. For further information, please contact Impact Publishers, P.O. Box 6016, Atascadero, CA 93423-6016, Phone: 1-800-246-7228. E-mail: sales@impactpublishers.com

Library of Congress Cataloging-in-Publication

Stewart, James W. (James Webster)
    Divorce handbook for California : how to dissolve your marriage
        without disaster / James W. Stewart. -- 5th ed.
            p. cm. -- (Rebuilding books, for divorce and beyond)
    Includes bibliographical references and index.
        ISBN 1-886230-52-8 (alk. paper)
        1. Divorce--Law and legislation--California--Popular works. I. Title.
        II. Series.

    KFC126.Z9 S74 2002
    346.79401'66--dc21

                                                            2002027638

Publisher's Note
This publication is designed to provide accurate and authoritative information in regard to the subject matter covered. It is sold with the understanding that the publisher is not engaged in rendering psychological, legal, or other professional services. If expert assistance or counseling is needed, the services of a competent professional should be sought.

Impact Publishers and colophon are registered trademarks of Impact Publishers, Inc.

Cover design by John Magee, San Luis Obispo, California
Printed in the United States of America on acid-free paper.
Published by **Impact Publishers, Inc.**
POST OFFICE BOX 6016
ATASCADERO, CALIFORNIA 93423-6016
www.impactpublishers.com

To my family with loving thanks for their support,
encouragement, and continued assurance that the information
was needed by anyone considering a divorce.

Acknowledgments

Thanks to Linda Diamond Raznick, Sue Koppett, and Mary Cottrell for their suggestions that have made this book more readable for the average person; and special thanks to my developmental editor/agent, Ward Winslow, who was willing to take a chance on an unpublished author who delivered his work written longhand on legal tablets.

J.W.S.
Palo Alto, California
July 2002

Contents

Foreword

Judge James Stewart has written a book many lawyers will love, but some won't. He didn't write the book for lawyers, though. He wrote it for their clients. And every client who has something to lose in a divorce will have something to gain from reading this book.

Perhaps the most valuable service Judge Stewart provides is some very practical guidance for the selection of a lawyer. But the value of this book won't end with the selection of a lawyer, at least for those clients who want to fully understand the decisions that need to be made. Lawyers who believe in encouraging such full understanding may want to provide their clients with a copy of Judge Stewart's book. It offers lucid and objective answers to all the questions divorce clients normally ask, and many more they should ask.

Bookstores abound with guides for handling one's own divorce, but there aren't many books written to guide the vast majority of divorce clients represented by lawyers. It's appropriate that such a book be authored by a judge with a depth of experience on both sides of the bench. That experience includes seeing many couples dissipate everything they've worked for in needless contentiousness. Judge Stewart is well known for his patience and creativeness in guiding difficult cases to a settlement.

One doesn't have to know many lawyers to realize two distinct styles pervade the practice of law. Some lawyers perceive their role as a hired fountain of wisdom commissioned by the client. The client's role is to provide the necessary information and money to finance the case. The lawyer's role is to make all the decisions and deliver the hoped-for result. Other lawyers believe in a client-centered approach to lawyering, in which more decisions are left to the client after the lawyer has fully explained all the risks and ramifications of various alternatives.

There are obvious advantages and disadvantages to both styles. Many clients prefer to turn decisions over to a lawyer they trust. After all, they've never been down the tortuous path of litigation before, and the lawyer has lots of experience to draw upon. And since the lawyer's meter is running by the minute, they see detailed explanations as an expensive luxury they can do without. Since they have to live with the outcome, other clients feel they want more control of the course of the litigation. Many decisions may turn on nonlegal considerations the lawyer does not and cannot fully appreciate.

These differences in style and client preference are not unique to the legal profession. The same differences are encountered in medicine and other learned professions.

Although it is good that clients have a choice, the reality is that too often the choice is blind. Clients don't know the questions they need to ask to make sure they are getting a lawyer whose style they can accept.

Offering an honest and realistic assessment of how cases are resolved, Judge Stewart's advice to clients will be welcomed by lawyers whose goal is to achieve a fair resolution that both sides can live with as quickly as possible. That doesn't include all divorce lawyers, however, and those who insist on being in full charge of a case may resent a client's query why their course of action differs from Judge Stewart's advice. Often, such lawyers leave an unhappy client in their wake. By providing a perspective that includes the long-term consequences of a divorce, Judge Stewart offers the client an opportunity to raise questions that need to be asked *before* decisions are made. Regardless of who makes those decisions, lawyer or client, having this information readily available can only contribute to greater client satisfaction with the outcome. Thus, although Judge Stewart's book was written for clients, the beneficiaries will certainly include many lawyers who value client satisfaction.

Gerald F. Uelmen, Former Dean
Santa Clara University School of Law
Santa Clara, California

Introduction

If you are separated from your spouse, or are merely contemplating a divorce, and your torment and anger are so great that your only goal is to inflict pain on that individual, then don't continue to read this book. It will not help you realize your goal.

If, on the other hand, your goal is to terminate a marriage in a manner in which you receive in property or support the amount to which you are legally entitled, or a lesser amount if you believe this will adequately meet your needs, then I can be of help. My advice may prevent you from spending far more than you can afford, regardless of your income or that of your spouse or the size of your joint estate. If you are really concerned about the best interests of your children, what you learn may spare them agony, devastation, and the permanent psychological damage that precludes them from forming successful relationships of their own.

This is not one of those how-to-do-it-by-yourself books that extols the virtues of mediation and suggests you don't need legal representation. This book is not an attack on matrimonial lawyers as a bunch of thieves and crooks, although the bar may perhaps perceive some of my remarks as attorney bashing. I believe you probably need the services of an attorney if you have anything worth preserving, including the right to request support at an unspecified future date.

Henceforth, I will use the word *dissolution* in place of *divorce*. Divorce is the more popular term when referring to the termination of a marriage, but it carries concepts that are no longer viable under California law, not the least of which is fault or blame.

2 Divorce Handbook for California

No-fault divorce statutes in California speak of "dissolution," although I am aware, in common parlance, you would never ask anyone if he or she had been "dissolved." Likewise, I shall use *spousal support* rather than *alimony*. The former is the word now used by our statutes and is free of connotations of a bygone era. Support is no longer thought of as a welfare handout sought by only one gender. It no longer contains the pejorative inference that alimony sparks in our minds.

My choices of dissolution and spousal support are not mere legal niceties. If you are to profit from this book, you must be persuaded to lay aside the outmoded beliefs conjured up by outdated words such as *divorce* and *alimony*.

The importance of a dissolution in your life cannot be underestimated, and the importance may well increase with the length of the marriage. Surely, a dissolution is a more important event than the purchase of a home and an event at least as crucial as a major career decision. The outcome of your dissolution action may well determine whether you will ever own a home (or another home) and whether you will have any assistance in training for a post-dissolution career. A dissolution is important even to those whose sole objective is to inflict financial or psychic pain on their spouses, for their success in attaining that goal is diminished to the extent they are denied things to which they are legally entitled or are left unnecessarily penniless.

The risk you run as you enter dissolution negotiations or litigation is that the attorneys you and your spouse hire, at $175 to $400 per hour, and the experts they retain to establish certain crucial facts, will erode the community property estate (and even one party's separate estate in some cases) to such an extent that you will receive substantially less in property and support than you would have received had you not hired a lawyer, or had you accepted your spouse's first offer.

Stated another way, you run the very real risk of obtaining less by using an attorney and a stable of experts than you could have obtained on your own. If, early on, your spouse offered you what you believed to be 40 percent of a $250,000 estate, you are not better off getting 50 percent of a $175,000 estate after attorneys and experts have consumed $75,000 in attorney fees and costs. The purpose of this book is to give you sufficient knowledge to get the 50 percent to which you are legally entitled without paying fees and costs so great they make winning an illusion.

Indeed, it is entirely possible the amount you receive above the other party's first unreasonable offer will be less than the fees and costs you pay an attorney. In other areas of legal litigation, this result either is not tolerated or is far less likely. The contingency fee reduces this risk in personal injury litigation. You pay your attorney a percentage of what is collected; if nothing is collected, you don't pay. Even here it is theoretically possible to receive less in recovery after fees and costs are paid than was offered by the insurance company before you hired counsel.

The insurance industry would have you believe this happens quite often. It doesn't. If you ask your matrimonial attorney to accept as a fee a percentage of what he or she obtains for you in net assets (after payment of all costs) over and above what your spouse has offered, your attorney would decline. The attorney might try to convince you that such an agreement would not be in your best interest. In reality, it is not in your attorney's best interest. Such an arrangement in a dissolution case may also violate the Rules of Professional Conduct promulgated by the State Bar.

It is true that in business litigation it is not unusual for the losing party to pay attorney fees and receive nothing in return. The possibility of loss, however, is a calculation usually made by businesspeople with a sharp eye on the cost-effectiveness of the litigation. Traumatized or emotionally battered spouses are unlikely to possess such judgment; and even if they do, they don't know the right questions to ask their attorneys. Matrimonial litigants are no better equipped than persons charged with a crime to protect their assets from the legal system. Indeed, it is also in the criminal law arena that substantial fees are paid unwisely to some attorneys who plead their clients guilty and obtain from the judge little more than the clients could have obtained on their own.

If I am to help you protect your life savings during your dissolution, you must discard certain myths that may have been true in California as late as the 1960s, but no longer apply today. These myths will be attacked in later chapters. Indeed, much of this book is written on the premise that a rejection of these myths is the most effective way to protect your assets in dissolution litigation.

Let me state eight of these myths here so you can begin to think about them.

- **Myth:** By hiring a lawyer with skill and ability far surpassing what my spouse can afford, I can effectively prevent my spouse from receiving what otherwise would be due under California law.

- **Myth:** My case ultimately will go to trial before a judge who will rule on the disputes my spouse and I cannot resolve.

- **Myth:** If my spouse is foolish enough not to hire an attorney, it will be to my benefit.

- **Myth:** If my lawyer hires the best experts available to support the claims of value of our property most favorable to my case, it will be to my economic benefit. We will start at extreme figures but will settle on more reasonable ones that are still weighted in my favor. At worst, the judge will compromise at a figure between my experts and my spouse's experts.

- **Myth:** The judge is the person with the most influence over which of us will have primary custody of our children.

- **Myth:** It is not possible to predict what a judge will award as temporary or permanent child or spousal support.

- **Myth:** My spouse can easily conceal assets; if that happens, I'll be out of luck later when I discover what was hidden.

- **Myth:** The judge who hears my case will have substantial experience in dissolution matters.

If you believe these myths, you will take an unnecessarily adversarial position in your dissolution case. You will focus on a trial that will never occur. You will believe an attorney who talks about "what we can get at trial." You will try to hire an unreasonably expensive lawyer who has a reputation as a heavy hitter. Your expensive lawyer will hire experts with the same reputation. The meter will tick at $175 to $500 per hour for attorneys and experts. Each expert will prepare a long report and will be deposed under oath for hours, if not days. You will lose a bundle of money unnecessarily, and the loss may well be so ruinous as to affect your standard of living for years to come. Such a loss of savings may well be more devastating to the wife because women generally have less earning capacity in our society and cannot as easily make up the loss as the husband can.

I hope you will reject these myths and persuade your spouse to read this book. I hope each of you will hire competent counsel, and will keep your counsel on a very short leash. And I hope you'll find in this book the information and encouragement you need to help you achieve a satisfactory settlement without financial — or other — disaster.

PART
I

HOW TO APPROACH YOUR DISSOLUTION

1

Why Divorce in California Is So Expensive

As the presiding judge of the Family Law Department for Santa Clara County Superior Court, it was my duty to preside over approximately six settlement conferences four days a week. In most California counties, the settlement conference is set a week or so before the case is scheduled for trial. Judges generally believe — often correctly — that obstreperous litigants will not seriously discuss settlement unless an illusory trial date is imminent.

The Cost of a Settlement Conference

If your case is not settled long before this settlement conference, you will suffer a big financial loss. Moreover, the conference is a devastating experience. You will probably be excluded from discussions with the settlement judge. You will probably be expected to discuss the most personal details of your life in a crowded hallway outside the courtroom, without the benefit of a private conference room. The attorneys will emerge from the settlement conference and tell you the judge's thinking on each disputed issue. You become certain the judge is more interested in settlement than in justice. Your attorney may then tell you it is pointless to go to trial because the judge who has just told you informally what the results will be, is also the judge who will preside at a trial of the case.

This is not true in all California counties, but the California Judicial Council is encouraging all counties to adopt the direct or federal system of calendaring, whereby the same judge hears every aspect of the case, including at least one or two difficult issues raised in the settlement conference.

If you do not settle, your attorney may warn you that when the issue of attorney fees arises after all other issues are resolved, the other side will tell the judge about the proposed settlement you rejected, and you may well be punished financially when the judge decides who pays whose attorney how much. If the case doesn't settle after the judge's first proposal, the attorneys will be called back into chambers, and the judge will increase the pressure for settlement by asking who is being unreasonable. Judges may or may not alter their first proposal before sending the attorneys back into the hallway for further discussions with you and your spouse. In counties such as Alameda County, where for years virtually no cases went to trial, a settlement conference can last one or two days. Judges view a marathon conference as a more efficient use of court time than a trial, because they can be holding four or five other settlement conferences while you are negotiating in the courthouse corridor.

In fourteen years of settlement conferences, I've seen the following scenario repeated over and over. The parties arrive at a settlement conference a week before the trial date. The attorneys have not seriously discussed settlement, but they have their experts in tow, often a forensic certified public accountant whose meter is running at $250 per hour or more, in addition to the attorney's $225–$600 per hour meter. The marriage is normally "lengthy" as defined by statute: over ten years. There are two children over whose custody the parties initially quarreled, but whose custody has now been resolved. They have an equity in their home of about $350,000 (modest for California). The husband has a small business or professional practice whose value is in dispute, but is worth $75,000 at most. His pension has a community property value of $25,000. The major unresolved issues are support for the wife and the value of the business.

The experts each have been deposed the better part of a day. At each deposition, the two attorneys were earning about $300 per hour and the expert a comparable amount, often portal-to-portal. The attorneys' fees have reached $125,000 ($200,000 if custody is still in dispute) and the experts' fees are $35,000. The experts' fees may be secured by liens on the residence, and the attorneys also may look to that asset for payment of fees.

Litigation has meant financial ruin for the parties. The attorneys and the experts have done well and are prepared to turn to other cases needing their attention at $350 per hour or more. The parties, when asked whether they would have settled the case at whatever their spouse had offered earlier in the process, had they known of the fees and costs a failure to settle would entail, answer with a resounding yes. But it is too late.

You can vary the length of the marriage by a few years, increase or decrease the estate, add or subtract a custody dispute, change the experts involved (psychotherapists in place of CPAs), but the result is what Family Court judges see daily: fees and costs that have eroded the parties' savings. If one believes, as some commentators do, that the experts and attorneys are engaged in a conspiracy to plunder the estate, it is possible to envision the marital estate as a giant plodding creature: killed by leeches and plucked clean by buzzards, it topples over while the predators turn to another meal.

But the conspiracy notion is simplistic and false. True, the litigation should have been settled much earlier when the fees were less than $40,000. The attorneys probably did not spend sufficient time in settlement negotiations in the early stages of the litigation. But they represented their client to the best of their ability and genuinely saw the spiraling fees as the other spouse's or other attorney's fault. Although the disaster could have been avoided, it was not intentional. It is worth noting, however, that any experienced Family Court judge will tell you that certain lawyers seem to have more than their fair share of cases that turn out profitably for them but are financial disasters for their clients. These attorneys are more neglectful than others, not necessarily more greedy.

It is also worth noting that judges never see the thousands of cases that settle amicably out of court; thus, our perceptions are skewed by the fact that we see the worst. But if I am correct in contending that litigation up to the settlement conference means financial ruin for the parties, the economic and social impact is heavy even for a county as large as my own — Santa Clara, California's fourth largest county. I have presided over 24 financial disasters per week, or 1,250 per year. Although that is a small portion of the dissolution actions filed in Santa Clara County each year, they have a severe impact on those who have assets worth fighting over. These financial disasters are a significant portion of total cases filed, in family court. Many of the 8,600 filings (excluding District Attorney paternity and support filings) result in either a reconciliation or a settlement in which little is divided beyond some furniture and a couple of automobiles with scant value.

The Impact of No-Fault

There are two theories commonly espoused by attorneys when discussing why dissolution is so expensive in California. The first theory places the blame on the requirement that community property be equally divided. Under this theory, it is thought that the California Legislature surely did not intend that a dissolution should be so expensive when it adopted the no-fault concept in 1970. Indeed, it was widely believed a no-fault approach would reduce the cost of litigation because the parties would not spend time in court arguing over who had been mentally or physically cruel, or who had committed adultery. The personal conduct of the parties would be irrelevant except in the small percentage of cases in which child custody was in dispute.

But the Legislature didn't simply adopt no-fault; it combined it with a requirement that community property be equally divided between the parties, down to the penny. A judge whose ruling goes against this requirement commits reversible error. Keep in mind we are discussing error by a judge in a ruling, not what the parties may legally agree to on their own. The parties are under no obligation to divide the property equally or in any other way. However, the combination of the no-fault concept with the requirement of an exactly equal division of community property has turned out to be the "California Full Employment Act" for matrimonial lawyers and the experts who assist them in trial preparation.

Prior to California's adoption of the no-fault concept, the judge would determine which party was free from blame or fault (if either was) and would award that party from one-half to all of the community property, depending on the egregiousness of the other party's conduct. The party guilty of extreme mental or physical cruelty, or adultery, was often awarded a lesser part of the property or none. The court, with such latitude for using discretion, needed only a general idea of the value of items that were all or partly community property: the home, the business or practice, the pension.

The enactment of no-fault legislation had the desired effect of reducing the mudslinging normally associated with fault divorce. But the equal-division requirement turned the focus from the parties to an evaluation of the property. The intelligent dissolution litigant was quick to conclude, "If I can inflate the judge's perception of the value of property awarded to my spouse and reduce the judge's perception of the value of property awarded to me, I can make a tidy profit as reimbursement for all the years of torment I was subjected to." So the attorney for the litigant retains experts whose opinions will be as desired. Of course, the other spouse's attorney is instructed to seek expert evaluations with opinions consistent with that spouse's views of reality (if not reality, what might be reasonably "sold" to a judge who is not an expert in the field). The expert, or evaluator, has now become the center of the litigation. Each expert has been consulted, deposed, and, of course, brought to the settlement conference to address the judge.

Judges, fearful of suggesting a settlement in which one party gets more than half of the community property, listen carefully to the experts. If still in doubt, they appoint their own experts and order the parties to pay the bill. Before no-fault/equal-division, experts normally were psychotherapists used in child custody litigation. Now CPAs and business opportunity brokers are needed to value businesses. Realtors and certified appraisers are called on to value homes and commercial real estate. Actuaries are used to put a present-day value on pensions to be received at a later date. Auction houses and furniture dealers are in demand to value furnishings. Even jewelers are occasionally needed to value fine jewelry, if, for example, a husband claims the wedding ring or other items were not really gifts but heirlooms that were to remain in his family or, at least, be treated as community property.

A whole subclass of professionals, practicing their profession in nontraditional ways, began to emerge under the no-fault/equal-division system. We had always had forensic mental health professionals who earned more income consulting to parties in child custody litigation than in the clinical practice of psychotherapy. In domestic litigation, suddenly CPAs with forensic skills were in demand. No one cared whether they could give competent tax advice or adequately prepare tax returns. Family law attorneys were far more interested in their ability to persuade the judge that a business or professional practice was worth a given sum. It was dissolution law, not the tax code, with which the CPA needed to be familiar.[1] Some forensic CPAs ceased giving tax advice or preparing returns, or delegated such menial work to drones in their office. Certain actuaries began to limit their work to pension evaluation in dissolution actions. Indeed, they began to develop reputations as husband-biased or wife-biased, depending on the calculations they used in putting a value on the community property portion of what was more often the husband's pension. Naturally, the presence of two experts with different bottom-line figures of value begot more litigation as attorneys argued for the judge to accept the opinion of the actuary favorable to their clients. The actuary, certified public accountant, or real property appraiser for the husband seldom agreed with the figures submitted by their counterparts on the wife's side. Experts who wanted to be hired again by the same law firm had better be reliable; that is, they could be depended on to tilt somewhat in favor of the position of the party whose attorney hired them. Actuaries developed reputations for favoring one side or the other, depending on whether, in placing a present value on a spouse's pension to be received years later, the actuary included reasonably anticipated salary increases the pensioner-spouse would likely receive before retiring.

Including such increases in the calculation substantially inflates the value of the pension at the time of dissolution. Such an approach is normally hostile to the interests of the pensioner-spouse (usually the husband) who is apt to have the entire pension and business awarded to him as an offset against some asset the other (nonpensioner)

---

[1] A 1989 California law requires judges to consider the tax consequences of their orders. Thus, the forensic CPA must now use the tax code in persuading a judge what level of spousal support should be set in light of the tax shelters available to both parties.

spouse (usually the wife) receives, such as the family home. The greater the value of the pension (and business), the more equity in the family residence the other spouse receives without having to pay cash to the pensioner-spouse.

Settlement conference judges, knowing the experts are tilting toward their clients' positions, then appoint the court's expert at additional cost to the parties. This is often an act of compassion. Judges know each expert's figures are inflated or deflated as the case may be. They want a compromise figure to lessen the economic devastation to one party that will occur if either expert's figure is accepted. But judges cannot simply pick a compromise figure unless there is some evidence (testimony) in the record that validates it. Appointment of an independent expert gives judges the opportunity to get such evidence into the record.

An independent expert almost always arrives at a figure someplace between those of the experts hired by the partisans. Thus, the appointment of an independent expert, however costly to the parties, allows the settlement judge to recommend a figure that will have legal validity in the remote chance the case should go to trial. The appointment will almost always assure settlement of the case so a trial is avoided. But court-appointed experts' fees, and the cost to depose them, may equal trial fees and costs. And, as discussed earlier, if the case is not settled long before a settlement conference, it can be a financial disaster for the parties as 80 percent or more of the total fees have already been charged.

The consumers in this system, the persons caught in the hurt endemic to the termination of a marriage, are asked to pay for these experts. And it is doubtful these experts give them any advantage in the outcome of the litigation (so long as both sides have an expert, and they almost always do). And it is a virtual certainty any advantage obtained will be less than the funds spent to pay the experts and the costs of litigation generated by their presence. In Chapter 4, I present some concrete recommendations on how you might avoid paying for numerous experts on multiple issues, whether they be your own, the judge's, or perhaps even your spouse's. As a consumer, you can at least try to protect yourself against the pillage of your marital property. You may not be successful if your spouse is irrational or oblivious to expense. But the effort is worth a try.

Those who adopt the theory that the high cost of dissolution is related to the equal-division requirement often suggest that if we required no more than an equitable division of community property — as the vast majority of other states do — we could retain no-fault and reduce the cost of dissolutions. Then, it is thought, the judge need only have a rough approximation of the value of each item of property and could, in an equitable division, give a displaced 40-year-old homemaker with two minor children a slight advantage in property to compensate for the fact that her earning capacity will never equal that of her husband whose career she dutifully supported for so many years and whose earning capacity will continue to escalate while she takes a menial job and raises the children.

A brief review of the practices in other states, however, reveals that many of the equitable distribution states have a presumption of equal distribution. Thus, the judge awards the marital property equally in the vast majority of cases. Moreover, there is no evidence that divorce is any less expensive in equitable distribution states. Indeed, one could argue that by building into their law an element of uncertainty of outcome, these states encourage litigation rather than settlement. My view is that equal division does contribute, to some extent, to the high cost of dissolution in California, but there seems to be no better alternative so long as we keep dissolution within the court system.

The other theory offered to explain the high cost of dissolution in California is that the courts have continually expanded the definition of community property. It is often suggested the expansion has met the demands of women's groups. An examination of the history of community property case law in California gives some support to this view. Not until 1962 was the concept of a law practice as community property first mentioned in an appellate case, and then the comment was only in passing.[2] Not until 1969 was there a definitive statement that a law practice was community property and as late as 1974 a California appellate court felt it necessary to put the rule in a published case.[3]

Doctors also appear to have escaped the community property net for almost as long as lawyers. The concept of a medical practice as community property was enunciated in 1963,[4] but even then the court was able to duck the issue of whether good will was a community property component of a medical practice. Good will was confirmed as a component in 1969 and reaffirmed in 1974. Again, we see the expansion of community property coming about the time of the adoption of no-fault in 1970.

Further research puts the theory on shakier ground. No one has ever seriously disputed that a business interest, whether corporate, partnership, or sole proprietorship, is community property, including good will. This was assumed in the early 20th century and repeated regularly long before the adoption of no-fault.[5] It was not until 1976, well after the introduction of no-fault, that nonvested pensions were held to be community property, but evaluations of, or disputes over, pensions are not usually one of the more expensive aspects of a dissolution.

---

[2] *In re Marriage of Brawman* (1962) 199 C.A.2d 876.

[3] *In re Marriage of Lopez* (1974) 38 C.A.3d 93.

[4] *Fritschi v Teed* (1963) 213 C.A.2d 718.

[5] *In re Marriage of Burton* (1958) 161 C.A.2d 572.

Whether either of these theories is correct is not important for the reader. The fact is that under California's present system it is incredibly expensive to dissolve a marriage in litigation that is even slightly contested. And the longer you remain within that system, the greater the chance your property will be consumed by attorney fees and costs that far exceed what you gain financially by the litigation.

Do's and Don'ts

Do...

- Settle your case, if at all possible, long before the formal pretrial settlement conference.

Don't...

- Don't assume you can profit by hiring experts to inflate the value of all property likely to be awarded to your spouse and diminish the value of all property likely to be awarded to you. You will lose if this tactic delays settlement.

- Don't assume the judge can legally find the value of certain property to be a compromise between your expert's figure and your spouse's expert's figure.

2

Hiring an Attorney

The choice of counsel is probably the most important decision you will make during your dissolution. If you are fortunate enough to employ an attorney who is flexible, sensitive to costs, and oriented toward early settlement, you will have taken a major step in the protection of your estate from the ravages of domestic litigation. You may be fortunate to stumble on such an attorney, but to rely on luck is foolish. If you wish to obtain a lawyer appropriate for your dissolution, you will have to search. (Even then, of course, you could make a serious mistake, but your chances of success are better.)

Selecting an Attorney

I suggest you interview at least four lawyers — more if you still have unresolved doubts. Some lawyers will give you one free consultation, others may not. Those who do not will likely charge you their hourly rate, so expect to pay between $225 and $600. It is well worth it to pay what is a small percent of the total fee in an effort to choose the correct attorney. It may ultimately save you as much as $150,000.

How you obtain the names of these four attorneys is important. It is risky to act on the touting of an attorney by your barber, hairdresser, neighbor, or co-worker. Some people have a need to brag that their attorney is the best; others are never satisfied with the work of the most competent practitioner. This is especially true of domestic litigation where clients tend to be result-oriented. Clients who believe they won may consider their attorney the best, regardless of how well or poorly the case was presented.

On the other hand, if you are acquainted with someone whose perception and judgment you trust and who claims to have received good representation, by all means consider that attorney. But you should never drop an attorney from consideration because an acquaintance was dissatisfied with the service. During domestic litigation, a person's judgment is often adversely affected by fear, anxiety, and anger. To such a person, no outcome will be satisfactory.

One other helpful resource: at least two names of attorneys you interview should come from names provided by your local bar association.

The Attorney-Client Interview

If you approach the first attorney-client interview cowed and intimidated by the attorney's status or reputation, or with the notion that this particular attorney is the only person who can competently represent you, your chances of selecting an appropriate attorney are minimal. You must take the attitude that the attorney will be charging you a high hourly fee, and you have the right to ask reasonable questions. If you are gracious and polite, you will not be seen as a problem client.

In the initial interview, you should feel free to take notes. In the solitude of your home, you can review these notes and ask yourself, "Did this attorney really answer my questions?" Even if you believe the attorney genuinely tried to answer your questions but you did not understand the answers, this should tell you something. Do you want to go through the litigation not understanding what your attorney is telling you? Moreover, it is not *your* job to be conversant with legal terms or to be better educated or worldly. It is *the attorney's* job to explain important concepts to you regardless of your background. Above all, do not decide to hire an attorney during the initial interview. A hasty decision will eliminate your opportunity to reflect calmly on your choice and, perhaps, your ability to interview other attorneys.

Certified Versus Noncertified Practitioners

Another difficult question is whether you should limit your list to attorneys *certified* as specialists in family law by the California State Bar. As a general rule, this is a good idea, at least for three of the four attorneys you interview. Certified specialists have passed a fairly rigorous examination in family law to obtain certification and are required to take a given number of hours of instruction each year to keep their knowledge of the law current. There may be some validity to the excuse that "I have avoided certification because I enjoy other types of litigation and do not wish to hold myself out as a specialist in one field." But before you accept this rationalization, you should know that attorneys can be certified to verify their knowledge, without publicizing it in a way that might limit their practices. Ask in what other fields the attorney practices and what percentage of his or her work is family law. If the other fields are a laundry list of most types of law, or the family law proportion is less than 60 percent, beware. To obtain your business, the attorney may have inflated the percentage, and you may be in danger of hiring a dabbler.

Attorneys who dabble in dissolution matters are to be avoided. They are probably not current in the law, or familiar with local practices and the biases and preferences of particular local judges. Worse, they either *think* they are aware of these things or believe such knowledge is unimportant. Some older attorneys may believe they can dabble in family law. Until the mid-1970s, many attorneys, including myself, handled an occasional divorce case. It was a relatively simple field, and the occasional divorce paid the office overhead and often led to a referral in what was then considered to be more important litigation.

Today, attorneys cannot dabble in family law for any period of time and remain free of malpractice accusations. With the advent of equal-division statutes wherein equality must be achieved in light of certain immediate tax consequences, family law may now be the most complicated area of litigation. Because of the complications created by our laws, you need an attorney competent in pension or business evaluation, characterization, and distribution of property. The expertise of a certified specialist is backed by the California State Bar. You should place on the nonspecialist the burden of proving his or her experience. If an attorney says anything like, "I don't normally handle divorce cases, but I'll do this as a favor to … ," run out of the office!

Reversing Some Myths

Let me return for a moment to three of the myths noted in Chapter 1. I want to turn them around so that they are positive statements of reality rather than untruths.

Realistically, you cannot gain a significant advantage in litigation by hiring a more skillful attorney than the attorney your spouse can afford. (The very premise, that the more one pays in fees the better the attorney one attains, is completely flawed.) Under California law — indeed, the law of most states — if your spouse needs help with attorney fees and costs and your greater income or asset base enables you to help your spouse with those fees, the judge will order you to do so. Moreover, as the spouse with more ample means, you may be ordered to make a substantial payment to your spouse's attorney at the outset of litigation so your spouse can litigate as fully as *your* intensity requires.

A description of a lawyer as a good lawyer probably is misleading if the reference is to skill and competence. Almost all certified specialists are good lawyers. The issue is not mere competence but whether your and your spouse's attorneys will line their pockets unnecessarily at the expense of you and your spouse. A grasp of reality requires that you understand it is not just your spouse's lawyer who has a hand in your pocket and will be paid from a portion of the estate the two of you have accumulated during the marriage. Your own attorney also is in the pay line, along with a host of experts if your estate is complex and sizable and the litigation is sufficiently intense. The bottom line is your attorney is not likely to obtain more for you than that to which you are reasonably entitled and will not drive the opposing side off the field of battle. You don't need that mythical heavy hitter. What you need is a competent attorney who will obtain for you that to which you are entitled by law in the shortest time possible.

Put aside the notion that your attorney is a great courthouse advocate whose skill and ability will hypnotize the judge. As discussed earlier, your case is not going to trial before a judge — short of a miracle; if it does, it will be a financial catastrophe for you. Santa Clara County averages approximately 8,600 family law filings per year. Although a significant number of these may proceed to a hearing of 30 minutes or less on such issues as support, attorney fees pending trial, or certain required injunctions, fewer than 1.5 percent go to a hearing that could even remotely be characterized as a trial. Under pressure from judges and a congested court system, cases settle. Even custody disputes normally settle. In the last two years, however, custody cases have begun going to trial in larger numbers. A recent California Supreme Court decision has given custodial parents the almost unfettered right to relocate the children across the country or in another state, depriving the other parent of frequent — in some cases, any — contact with the children. The fear of losing one's children in a cross-country move has increased custody trials for reasons that will be explained at length in Chapter 7 on child custody.

Finally, encourage your spouse to obtain competent counsel. It is almost impossible to settle a case with someone who lacks legal advice. Cases settle when both sides conclude that a settlement gives each side about what each would obtain if the case were decided by a judge. The self-represented litigant who appears *in propria persona* (usually just *pro per*) has no knowledge of the law against which to measure your offer, and hence no idea of whether a proposed settlement is reasonable or not. The case may settle if the unrepresented spouse is willing to settle for what he or she needs, even if legally entitled to more. But spouses seldom take such a position, if for no other reason than it is not very intelligent to give away one's property. A case in which one party is *in pro per* is difficult to settle. Not only are *pro pers* reluctant to settle a case because they have no idea whether or not a proposed settlement is fair in light of applicable law, but *pro per* litigants may also engage in inappropriate conduct they do not know is inappropriate or believe they can get away with.

Pro per litigants may seek to dispose of community funds, move back into the family residence exclusively occupied by their spouse for several months, or demand joint custody or excessive visitation in situations in which their wishes would never be approved by a judge. Thousands of dollars can be lost to the parties while a *pro per* refuses a reasonable settlement or acts out emotions in what seems like an endless temper tantrum that a competent attorney would not tolerate. Once represented, a former *pro per* can obtain reasonable legal advice on how to evaluate a settlement proposal. If inappropriate conduct continues, a good attorney will suggest that unless it stops the party will again be without counsel. With even more telling effect, an attorney will explain to the *pro per* that, to bring the inappropriate conduct under control, the court will award the other party the fees charged by that party's attorney for responding to such conduct. That's usually an attention-getter.

Moreover, if you are represented by an attorney and your spouse is not, that fact increases the chance that whatever settlement agreement you are able to arrive at will later be set aside by a court. In California it is relatively easy to set aside an agreement (and the judgment that makes the agreement a court order) that is unfair to one party up to one year after entry of the judgment. One need only show a mistake of law or fact on the part of the aggrieved party. After one year, it becomes very difficult to set aside the agreement and judgment because the aggrieved party must show "extrinsic fraud," which means that by fraud or trickery or for some other reason related to the other party's conduct, the aggrieved party was actually denied the right to be heard in court. The chances of an agreement and judgment being set aside either before or after the one-year period are enhanced if the aggrieved party was unrepresented and the other party had counsel.

What to Avoid

If you want cost-effective representation, there are certain attorneys and certain practices you need to avoid.

Divorce Mills. No matter how competent the representation may be, avoid the "divorce mill": an attorney or a group of attorneys who rely on numerous paralegals or other attorneys to prepare a case for hearings or trial. Let's examine how a divorce mill typically handles a dissolution case.

Your initial interview is with the attorney to whom you were referred. Thereafter, the papers are prepared by a paralegal or staff lawyer as opposed to Mr. Big (or Ms. Big) with whom you interviewed. The interrogatories (questions asked of you by the other side, which must be answered under oath) are prepared by the staff attorney. Experts are interviewed and employed by the staff attorney. In the worst examples, even depositions are taken by staff attorneys. Court appearances, of course, are made by Mr. or Ms. Big. He or she may be well prepared, having reviewed the file in advance and discussed factual issues with the staff lawyer. Since Mr. or Ms. Big appears in court daily, armed with well-prepared files, he or she is not familiar with the particular file and thus is not able to discuss settlement intelligently when a hearing is not imminent. Spending the better part of each day in court, Mr. or Ms. Big does not have the time to review each file carefully and engage in settlement discussions with opposing counsel.

This attorney probably will not, and certainly should not, delegate settlement negotiations to a hireling whom you have not met and did not employ. Thus, your file is on a conveyor belt of preparation. It may well be competent preparation. Experts will be interviewed, retained, and deposed in an orderly fashion — at enormous hourly fees. But your case will not settle short of the settlement conference the week before the trial date. The conveyor belt is not programmed for you to discuss possible settlement offers that might be made to opposing counsel. Indeed, such an effort would interfere with its uninterrupted movement.

The conveyor-belt or divorce-mill approach may have been suitable in earlier days when a greater percentage of cases went to trial — days when one could confidently go to trial without an army of experts. Today, you need an attorney who will prepare your files with the help of no more than one paralegal or staff attorney, will be familiar with the day-to-day status of your case, will be prepared to discuss settlement at any time, and will initiate settlement discussions at reasonable intervals if the opposition fails to do so.

Even if you are satisfied that your prospective attorney is not running a mill, you may want to determine whether the attorney you retain will be the person who will accompany you to court for various motions and conferences. If you expect the attorney with whom you interviewed to be with you on those occasions, but find another attorney accompanying you, the result may be a crisis of confidence that could have been avoided by a clear understanding.

I want to clarify one point. An attorney cannot prepare for settlement. Your counsel cannot ignore discovery and research on the assumption a case will settle. The attorney must prepare for trial, and, indeed, may be justified in deferring settlement until basic discovery is complete. But if your dissolution is to be cost-effective, your attorney must be willing to make reasonable settlement offers, early and at sensible intervals thereafter while preparing for trial. Only in this way can the attorney protect your legal position and your pocketbook.

Excessive Nonrefundable Fees. Attorneys who appear to overreach on their fee arrangements should also be avoided. When attorneys talk about a retainer fee over $3,500 as being nonrefundable, it is time to leave that office. It is true that they are using the word *retainer* in its traditional sense: a fee paid to insure an attorney's availability to represent you, for which you receive no credit against hourly charges and which is not refundable. Today, however, family lawyers who care about their client's well-being do not charge large, nonrefundable fees of $10,000 to $15,000. They charge a retainer fee, paid at the outset and credited against charges for future work. When the retainer fee has been used up, you are expected to keep your bill current. If $3,500 or less of your retainer fee is nonrefundable, this is probably a legitimate way for the attorney to be certain that you are serious about proceeding with the case.

A large nonrefundable fee places you in a situation where it would be highly detrimental to change attorneys early on, even though you have concluded you made a serious mistake. Do not accept the specious argument that a nonrefundable retainer motivates your attorney toward early settlement of your case (a quick profit for little work). Good attorneys don't need to profit financially to settle a case, and those in the nonrefundable crowd are generally not known for their ability to settle cases before the settlement conference. They are more likely to settle cases only when the client has run out of money.

You should also be skeptical of requests for a lien on your home to secure payment of fees. This may be appropriate in some instances, and is now approved by statute, but you should have independent legal advice. Such a lien can create a conflict of interest between you and your attorney. It might be in your best interests to purchase the family residence from your spouse, or to seek a deferral of the sale of the property. If your attorney is expecting to be paid out of escrow at the time of sale, you may lose sleep about whose interest is paramount in your attorney's mind.

Be aware that if you are without funds for a retainer, your attorney may be able to look to your spouse for the payment of a good portion of your fees. Before 1975, an attorney may have been justified in refusing to ask your spouse for compensation. Judges tended to award fees grudgingly, and then only after a case was terminated. Indeed, persons seeking an award of fees were made to feel as if they were seeking a welfare handout. In Chapter 13, I will more fully discuss a 1985 California Court of

Appeal decision establishing the up-front award of attorney fees as the norm rather than the exception. Perceptive judges realize the issue of early fees for the low earner is important to women's groups. Most capable attorneys will often agree to make a motion for fees from your spouse on the understanding they will not represent you if the motion is denied and you are unable to pay a retainer fee. Such motions are invariably granted when attorneys are prepared to look the judge in the eye and say they must decline to represent the client if sufficient funds are not available to allow competent representation.

Aggressiveness. Any reasonably alert client will be suspicious of the attorney who appears overly aggressive ("We'll haul his ass into court and get you a fair shake"), as well as an attorney who guarantees a given result. It is not improper, however, for an attorney to indicate you may be misinformed or uninformed as to the law. The attorney may be correct in advising you that, assuming a reasonable outcome, you may receive more in property or support than that to which you believed you were entitled.

Out-of-County Location. Another rule you should not violate: Never hire an attorney from a county other than that in which the case is to be filed, unless the county court is near the attorney's office and you are convinced he or she practices regularly before the judges of the court that will hear your case. So many decisions in family law are within the judge's discretion that attorneys must be familiar with the value structure of every judge who may hear a motion or conduct a settlement conference in your case. They must know a judge's attitude toward joint custody (equal time-sharing), working mothers, spousal support, needs of children, and a host of values that affect judicial decisions.

Perhaps a more important reason for hiring only an attorney who customarily practices in the county of filing is that the attorney will have established credibility with the judges of that county. All attorneys go through an initial period in which judges determine whether they can rely on what the attorney represents to be true. Those who achieve credibility with the bench have a distinct advantage in all litigation. Those who fail to do so carry an unspoken burden of proof throughout their careers. The former group tends to prevail in close or unclear situations. An attorney from another county will not have established credibility with local judges.

Although there are a few notable exceptions, quality family law attorneys seldom venture beyond one primary county of practice. They realize they are unfamiliar with local practices, local rules of procedure, and local judges. It is enough to keep track of changing personalities in one county. It simply cannot be done statewide, and clients should not pay for the time out-of-town attorneys spend educating themselves by consulting with the local attorneys the client should have hired.

Gender Bias. You should also not limit your search to male attorneys as some litigants do. There are at least two reasons why some persons feel more comfortable with a male attorney. Men often feel they can relate their most personal feelings to another man; that another man will be understanding of the husband's plight whereas a woman may not. If this is how you feel, then by all means hire a male attorney. However, if you are about to limit your search to male attorneys because you believe female attorneys lack the persuasive power and strength to negotiate a reasonable settlement or to persuade a judge at a settlement conference or trial, you are making a major mistake. This mistake is often made by the wife. She may carry an image of other women as weaker and less capable than men. This is often true of wives who have been traditional homemakers and lack confidence in their ability to function outside the home. Women who lack confidence in themselves often don't have confidence in other women.

Actually, unlike during the 1970s, women now compose a substantial portion of the family law bar in all major metropolitan areas of California. Their courtroom and negotiation skills are equal to those of male lawyers. To think only men can handle a tough battle is extremely naive. The work of women attorneys practicing family law is, on average, equal to that of their male counterparts. Their presence at the courthouse is so common that few judges are biased against them. Whatever residual sexist feelings judges may still harbor should not materially affect your case. Judges with gender bias quickly earn a reputation as such among local women attorneys, and are so few in number they can be avoided by discreet maneuvers or, as a last resort, by the use of a peremptory challenge: In California, each side has the right to remove one judge from the case without giving a reason. (See Chapter 6, Shopping for a Judge.)

Questions to Ask

Even the most perceptive person seeking to retain an attorney for dissolution litigation can make a mistake. But by asking a few probing questions, you should be able to determine whether you are in the presence of an experienced family law attorney or an attorney who occasionally dabbles in family law. Any experienced family law attorney should easily answer all of the following questions about *local dissolution procedures:*

1. Does the county have a self-contained family law division of judges familiar with dissolution law, or is a motion or trial apt to be heard by a judge with unknown family law experience?

2. Do the judges who regularly hear motions for spousal support normally consider income tax factors in deciding how much money is available for support? Do they receive into evidence computer printouts from programs that calculate the impact of certain tax shelters, or do they use their own computers to make the calculation?

3. Are there two or three actuaries in this county who evaluate pensions in the majority of dissolution cases? Which of these have you previously employed? Are you aware of which actuaries do or do not consider expected future salary increases in placing a present value on the pension to be received in the future?

4. Are there one or two appraisers or auction houses in this area that do most of the furniture evaluation in dissolution cases? (The attorney should either know them by name or at least name the person he or she uses most often.)

If your case involves an actual or potential custody or visitation dispute, you should be sure your prospective attorney can answer the following questions about *local custody procedures:*

1. In this county, do all judges refer custody disputes to mental health professionals to prepare a recommendation to the court?

2. Is there a court-connected mediation service in this county, or is mediation done by private mediators appointed by the judge?

3. Is mediation confidential, or will my statements or views be revealed to the judge by the mediator?

4. If mediation fails, does the mediator then do the evaluation of the custody dispute and make a report to the judge, or will the evaluation be done by someone other than the mediator?[1]

---

[1] Mediation and evaluation will be fully defined in later chapters. At this point, it is sufficient to say that mediation is the effort of a third party to get the litigants to agree. Evaluation is the process by which the evaluator actually makes a decision on who should have custody and asks a judge to adopt that decision. It is akin to arbitration.

Correct answers to these questions reveal a person capable of representing you in a custody or visitation dispute. (You should know the correct answers or how to find them after you have read this book.) An attorney who fails to respond correctly is not conversant with local procedures for determining custody.

In addition to asking a few questions to establish a prospective attorney's expertise, you should clarify the following points — and be sure they are clearly stated in the contract that you are asked to sign — regarding *attorney-client procedures:*

1. Will the attorney send you copies of all letters sent to or received from opposing counsel, and copies of all pleadings filed with the court so you can remain current on the status of your case?

2. Will the attorney personally return your telephone calls? Does the attorney normally return calls from clients the same day or the following day? (Obviously if the attorney is engaged in a trial it is reasonable for a paralegal or an associate to return your call. If the attorney is always in trial, you are in a mill.) Are there charges for telephone calls? If so, is there a minimum fee?

3. If your spouse's attorney files a pretrial motion and the attorney has another case that conflicts, who will accompany you to court if your spouse's attorney will not grant a continuance?

4. Will you be charged for secretarial time or does the attorney pay this as part of office overhead? For time spent talking to paralegals about the case?

5. Will your attorney be willing to suggest a settlement conference to opposing counsel as soon as you have made your data available? If not, will the attorney attempt to set up a conference as soon as preliminary discovery is complete? Will he or she commit to an early face-to-face settlement conference if that is agreeable to your spouse's attorney? Are you welcome in the room during settlement discussions, or will you be asked to remain in another area until your attorney can bring a proposal to you?

Finally, it might be wise to obtain the attorney's view of opposing counsel. Have they worked with one another before? Do they have a good working relationship? Is your spouse's attorney one who normally makes all reasonable efforts to settle a case? An attorney's relationship with opposing counsel may be important. If one prospective attorney finds your spouse's lawyer overly litigious, but others you interview find that attorney to be quite reasonable, you should keep that in mind. Unnecessary quarreling between counsel often results in skyrocketing attorney fees. That is not to suggest either your own or your spouse's counsel need compromise a single issue that is not in the client's best interest. It is to say, however, that the most intense litigation is always less costly if the attorneys have a respectful and courteous relationship.

Changing Attorneys

You may conclude the attorney you have retained is a poor choice. Your phone calls are not returned, you are refused discussions of a possible settlement offer, or you are not sent copies of correspondence with opposing counsel or pleadings filed with the court. Should you change attorneys? To change an attorney once will probably not prejudice your case. Even if the attorney you dismissed is highly respected by the judge, the change should not taint your case. Judges know there are any number of reasons you and your attorney may have parted company, and they are not likely to give the matter any thought.

On the other hand, a second, third, or fourth change of attorney will irreparably harm your case. Most judges believe persons who go through several attorneys during one dissolution often are neurotic or unreasonable. They are considered problem clients by the bar as well as by the judges. You will understand how badly a second or third change of attorney has prejudiced your case when you hear your spouse's attorney emphasizing in all pleadings and at oral arguments before the judge that your current lawyer is your "fourth." Such a statement carries with it the inference that you lack stability, or your demands are unreasonable, or both. If you absolutely must have a third attorney, I would suggest you try to associate him or her with your second attorney in what appears to the judge as a joint effort. If you have two attorneys of record, you can give the more recently retained attorney primary responsibility for the case. Of course, this ploy can succeed only if the attorney in whom you have lost confidence will permit an association and gracefully accept a minor role in the litigation. Cooperation or lack thereof is apt to be determined by whether or not you have paid for that attorney's services.

In changing attorneys, you should know that you have a right to your case file, including all pleadings and correspondence. The rules of the State Bar do not permit attorneys to withhold a file as ransom for payment of fees. Attorneys must, after reasonable time to make a copy of the file for their own records, turn the file over to you. Copying even the most voluminous of files should not require more than 72 hours.

DO'S AND DON'TS

Do...

- Interview at least four prospective attorneys before hiring one to represent you.

- Interview at least three certified family law specialists.

- Encourage your spouse to obtain promptly the most competent counsel available.

- Ask questions at the initial interview to determine the attorney's familiarity with local practices.

- Hire an attorney who will agree to discuss settlement early and at regular intervals thereafter.

- Allow your attorney to do some investigation and discovery before making a settlement offer.

Don't...

- Don't hire an attorney who asks for a large nonrefundable retainer fee.

- Don't rely on your barber, hairdresser, neighbor, or friend to designate more than one name out of four on your interview list. Obtain at least three from the County Bar Association.

- Don't hire an attorney who dabbles in family law or is taking the case as a favor to you or a mutual friend.

- Don't obtain a courtroom heavy hitter in the belief your case is going to trial.

- Don't hire an attorney connected with a divorce mill.

- Don't give an attorney a lien on your home or other real property without legal advice from an independent attorney.

- Don't limit your search to male attorneys.

- Don't hire an attorney from outside the county or the general area where the action is filed.

- Don't change attorneys more than once.

3

Bypassing the Public Courts

Although it is a shock to most laypeople, it is not uncommon for parties to a dissolution to opt entirely out of the public court system. How? By engaging a retired judge or a family law attorney to *mediate* and/or *arbitrate* the case. Obviously this cannot be done without the concurrence of both parties. Because the engagement of retired judges to hear lawsuits is a recent development, some explanation of the concept may be helpful.

Saving Big $$$: The "Rent-a-Judge" Option

Private arbitration or mediation before a retired judge is an idea that has become firmly established since the early 1980s as an adjunct to the public court system. Its rise in popularity has been nothing short of phenomenal. From its inception when two retired judges in Southern California offered their services to hear legal disputes, private judicial arbitration — or "rent-a-judge," as it is called — has grown into a multimillion-dollar industry in California and across the country. Large and small associations of retired judges have sprung up to provide arbitration and pro tem (temporary) judging as an alternative to the traditional court process. Large corporations and insurance companies, finding substantial financial savings from private judging, have begun to write arbitration proceedings by a given association of retired judges into their contracts and policies. Many retired judges are spending as much time deciding cases as they did before retirement — and certainly earning far more money.

Mediation and Arbitration Defined

Before explaining the benefits and problems of this process, I want to make clear what is meant by *mediation* and *arbitration.*

Mediation, as used in this chapter, means an effort by an independent person, referred to as a *mediator,* to bring the parties to a dissolution together in a settlement of all disputes. It is not a proceeding in which someone makes a ruling or a decision of any type. If a settlement is not reached, no effort is made to assess blame or to fault either party. It is confidential. The mediator will not reveal to a judge or other decision-maker what was said or what position on the issues either party took. If a settlement is reached, it is entirely voluntary. It is not reached because one or both parties feared criticisms or legal repercussions.

Arbitration is defined as a process whereby the person or persons referred to as the *arbitrator* makes a ruling in the matter as to all issues submitted by the parties for decision. In family law matters an arbitrator's rulings will set support, divide property, and on occasion determine access to children. The process is virtually indistinguishable from a trial before a judge, except that the rules of evidence need not be observed, the proceedings need not be reported, and they are usually not held in a public courtroom. However, as in a trial before a judge, each party has a right to present evidence, to cross-examine witnesses, and to be represented by counsel.

Private judges do both mediation and arbitration for an hourly fee.

Criticisms of Private Judging

The idea of hiring a retired judge to mediate or arbitrate a dispute that would normally go to trial in a court of law has created a firestorm of controversy. Its advocates see it as providing relief to a congested court system and financial savings to everyone who opts out of the public courts and into private judicial dispute resolution. Rent-a-judge detractors see it as instituting two tiers in our legal system: one for the rich who can afford to rent a retired judge and one for everyone else. They see it as a drain on judicial talent. They point out that some of our brightest judges are now retiring early so they can go into the more lucrative business of private judging. Finally, they raise some important ethical questions about private judging. How can a retired judge be impartial in an arbitration between a corporation and an individual or other business when the corporation has written the judge's arbitration association into its contracts as the arbiter of all disputes arising under the contract? The corporation, by making such a designation, is responsible for thousands of dollars of income to the judge and possibly hundreds of thousands to the judge's association.

Many cases go to a retired judge as an arbiter, mediator, or trial judge because one attorney has suggested the idea to the other side and they have agreed. This is especially true in family law cases where there are no contracts that predetermine how a dispute will be resolved. But suppose the attorney who has suggested using a particular retired judge has made a like suggestion in several other cases during the past year. That attorney has been directly responsible for substantial income earned by the judge that year. Can the judge be impartial in a case between that attorney and an attorney who has never been before the judge? It may be that the judge can be impartial. But, at a minimum, should not each attorney be informed of all prior litigation that any other attorney or party in the case has had before the retired judge, or the judge's association? Unlike in the early days of private judging, these disclosures are now required by law.

On the whole, I think that private judging by retired judges is an asset to the court system so long as such disclosures are made. Each case that is removed from the public court system allows other cases to proceed more rapidly to a conclusion, and the financial savings to the litigants are often substantial. Moreover, the award of the arbitrator can be made a judgment of the appropriate court.

Advantages to Private Judging in Family Law Cases

Private judging has always been more popular in Southern California, and especially in Los Angeles County, than in other parts of the state. In a county in which it used to take four years to get a civil case to trial, the demand for judges who could hear a matter within six months or so was overwhelming. Companies and individuals with experience in litigation know that early resolution of a case will save attorney fees and costs, as well as give certainty that allows financial planning for the future. If the early resolution is a fair settlement rather than a trial, the savings are even greater.

In Northern California, private judging did not balloon in popularity the way it did in the south. The counties of Northern California had civil calendars that are reasonably current and thus the wait for a trial was not nearly so long as in Los Angeles. However, over time, the use of private judges in Northern California has grown considerably and is now a major industry. Indeed, one retired judge had a private courtroom built when he undertook to hear a matter that lasted more than a year.

Private judging in family law cases has followed the same pattern as in other types of litigation. Unlike civil cases, however, the family law calendars are not greatly congested, so I am uncertain why private judging became so popular so rapidly. Perhaps trials tended to be continued or delayed, or attorneys sought to obtain a judge more experienced in family law than those judges assigned to family law cases. Indeed, the demand in Southern California grew so great that for a while retired judges from Northern California were commuting to the south on a weekly basis to meet endless requests for private judges.

In Northern California, private judging in family law matters did not have a similar burst of growth and popularity. Yet over time, the demand in the north for private judges to mediate or to act as a trial judge in family law matters has slowly increased. At present, however, most of the work is done by attorneys rather than retired judges. The reason for this is that there are very few retired judges in Northern California with recent experience in family law, and there is a great demand for them to sit in other types of cases. Indeed, many retired judges refuse family law cases because they find them distasteful. The scarcity of retired judges with extensive and recent family law experience has tended to stunt the growth of private judging by judges in Northern California family law cases. However, as time passes, the number of judges with extensive family law experience is increasing. Most clients are more comfortable agreeing that a case be heard by a retired judge than by an attorney in private practice.

Initially, the demand for private judges was limited to dissolutions involving the very affluent who could afford the expense of hiring a retired judge. Then some attorneys began to believe that almost all clients could actually save money by opting out of the public court process. A private judge can begin a case on time. The parties are not put on standby for trial for several days, paying all the while for experts to remain available on short notice. Trials are not stopped and restarted so that the judge can attend to duties on other cases. Finally, because family law judges are often the most recent appointees to the bench and may be assigned to hear domestic cases without prior experience, some attorneys feel that private judging avoids the chance of error by an inexperienced judge that could lead to a costly appeal.

In addition to financial savings, an early and certain date for a trial in a relaxed atmosphere may reduce wear and tear on everyone, and it certainly enhances the chance of settlement without a trial, and provides the parties with privacy.

Costs of Private Judging in Family Law

The major association established by retired judges to receive requests for private work is the Judicial Arbitration and Mediation Services, Inc., widely known as JAMS. Judges in this organization charge $500 to $1,200 per hour for their work in family law cases. However, there are numerous smaller groups of judges associated for the purpose of private judging, and many retired judges work alone. Because these smaller associations and individual judges do not have the overhead of a major organization such as JAMS, their fees may be somewhat lower. Moreover, the clients are not paying their attorneys to stand in the courthouse halls waiting for a courtroom to open up. These fees may be lower than those of attorneys engaged in private judging because attorneys have major overhead costs that can exceed 50 percent of their gross income.

Telephone numbers for associations of retired judges and for individuals engaged in private judging can normally be obtained from the county Superior Court from which the judges retired. Associations are often listed in the Yellow Pages under *Arbitrators*.

In summary, substantial savings may be realized by opting out of the public court system. Whether one uses a retired judge or a respected attorney, the benefits of staying far from crowded courtrooms and long calendars of cases competing for the court's time can be both financial and emotional. There is no good reason why you should not consider retaining a private judge to mediate your case in the hope of reaching an early settlement. If mediation fails, you may then want that judge to serve as an a trial judge and rule on disputed issues. All of your rights to appeal are preserved exactly as if you were in the public system. The *average* family law trial takes about less than a full day, and thus the cost is manageable, even if your trial takes up to two and one-half days. If the case is substantially longer because of complex issues, it usually indicates that the parties have the wherewithal to pay more. You and your attorney may wish to withhold consent for the retired judge to act as a trial judge in the case until you get a sense of the judge's objectivity, temperament, and knowledge of the law during the mediation process. If you are displeased, you can either retain another private judge or opt back into the public court system.

Mediation Before Filing Legal Action

Thus far in this chapter I have discussed bypassing the public court process entirely. Even if you choose not to opt out, I strongly suggest that you consider mediation before entering into court litigation. Attorney fees in California have reached prohibitive levels for upper-middle-class people. The average cost to each spouse of a simple dissolution — defined as one that settles without a trial and has no complex issues — now runs from $15,000 to $30,000. Dissolutions that entail complex issues involving experts such as CPAs or mental health professionals will easily cost each party between $125,000 and $250,000. Fees of $300,000 to $900,000 are not common, but judges see them occasionally.

Mediation prior to litigation represents a reasonable method by which parties to a dissolution can seek to protect their life savings from the erosion a contested dissolution brings. It is not opting out of the public court process; rather, it is an effort to settle litigation before attorney fees become exorbitant.

Who Should Be the Mediator?

It is a mistake to hire anyone other than an attorney or a retired judge to mediate your dissolution. A layperson will not understand the difficult legal issues that may arise. Moreover, parties are usually attempting to settle a case at or near what a court would order if the matter went to an expensive trial. In effect, the parties or their attorneys, if they are represented, will be attempting to convince the mediator that what they are requesting is exactly what a court would do on the various issues in dispute. A layperson simply does not have the training to evaluate what a judge would do in a given case.

Not any retired judge or practicing attorney will be able to mediate your case properly. You must have an attorney with extensive experience in family law or a retired judge with recent family law experience. Normally, it is safe to hire an attorney who is certified by the State Bar as a family law specialist. That attorney has passed a rigorous examination to obtain that designation. Recent family law experience for a judge does not mean that the judge has recently retired. Rather, it means that the judge keeps up on changes in family law by attending conferences and lectures held for that purpose and has heard several family law matters within the last year. Obviously the judge should have spent at least a year or so hearing family law cases in the five years prior to retirement. The extent of recent experience required will vary with the complexity of the case or the extent to which the case presents issues affected by recent changes in the law.

If you and your spouse are represented by attorneys, they should be familiar with any number of attorneys who have the necessary experience and reputation for fairness to qualify as mediators. If you are unrepresented, locating an attorney or retired judge is more difficult. The Yellow Pages will indicate which attorneys are certified family law specialists. Your County Bar Association may be willing to refer you to a certified specialist who may be qualified and willing to serve as a mediator, or who, at a minimum, should be able to provide a list of qualified attorneys.

If any issues to be mediated are related to child custody, the mediator for those issues should be a mental health professional, preferably holding a Ph.D. degree in psychology and/or licensed as a psychologist by the California state Board of Psychology. (Be aware that a doctorate in educational psychology obtained in a department of education rather than a department of psychology is not equivalent or adequate.) Your mediator should have extensive experience in making custody evaluations and should have a record of appointments by judges to do so. A family law attorney should know any number of qualified persons. If the attorneys cannot agree on someone, they can ask a judge to make an appointment. If you are without an attorney, you should purchase a half hour of time from a certified specialist whose name you should be able to obtain from the County Bar. The attorney should be able to refer you to a number of psychologists who are capable of mediating custody issues in your case.

However, before hiring a private psychologist to mediate a custody dispute, you should bear in mind that mediation is required by law in any case in which an issue related to a parenting plan for children is in dispute. This service is provided by the court free or for a nominal charge. By and large, persons employed by the court to mediate issues related to parenting are quite skilled and do a very good job. Their credentials may not match those of many private practitioners, and in some counties they are not required to be licensed. Although many of the people in private practice may be more qualified in terms of degrees held, there are private psychologists who are not as skilled as the mental health professionals available at no charge through the court. Thus, there is some risk in the selection of a mediator from the private sector without thoroughly screening the individual.

In the chapter on child custody, I discuss what is referred to as "muscle mediation." This is mediation that is not confidential and where the mediator will make a recommendation to the judge if the parties do not agree. Agreements reached under such coercion are not really voluntary and may not last. If you cannot obtain confidential mediation in the county where your dissolution is filed, you have a good reason to opt for a private mediator. The choice between private and court-provided mediation of custody issues is best made after a consultation with an experienced family law attorney.

Should You Be Represented by an Attorney at Mediation?

Many mediators believe that the parties to a failed marriage should attempt to resolve their differences in mediation before they retain counsel or file an action for dissolution. This certainly works for some people, and if an agreement is reached, the parties save enormous litigation costs. Although I feel that parties are almost always better off with an attorney, you may feel that retaining an attorney for mediation is not cost-effective.

If you choose to mediate without your own attorney, it becomes even more important to hire an experienced family lawyer as mediator rather than a layperson. As discussed above, most divorcing couples wish to settle their case on terms close to what the outcome would be if they proceeded through the court system. Yet one party may propose a settlement that is quite unfair in terms of the result that one might reasonably expect from a judge. If no one in the mediation has a working and current knowledge of family law, no one would be aware of the problem.

Protecting Yourself If You Mediate Without an Attorney

If you decide to mediate without an attorney, you can do several things to ensure that whatever settlement is reached is close to the result that is likely in court. You may wish to purchase an hour or so of an attorney's time before the mediation begins in order to understand your legal rights and the parameters of a fair settlement. You should advise the attorney that if the mediation fails and litigation is commenced, you will be represented by someone else. The attorney will then understand that the failure of the parties to reach an agreement will not result in litigation fees, and thus any incentive to be overly critical or litigious is removed. It is absolutely mandatory that this attorney also review and approve any settlement reached before you execute the written agreement.

The parties may also wish to agree with the mediator that they will be advised if the mediator believes that a proposal on any issue would award one party significantly more or less than might be expected from a court decision. The parties may still wish to settle the issue on those terms. An advantage to a spouse on one issue is often offset by an advantage to the other spouse on another issue. For example, a waiver of spousal support after a long marriage might be exchanged for a greater share of the community property. The important thing is that the parties know when they have strayed beyond the parameters of a likely outcome in court.

When Never to Mediate Without Counsel

If one spouse is at a significant disadvantage in the negotiation process, that spouse should never mediate without counsel. One reason divorcing parties retain attorneys is to equalize negotiation skills. For example, one spouse may have consistently been overwhelmed by the other in disputes occurring during the marriage. Or the parties may not have equal knowledge of their income or assets. This is most glaring when a successful businessman or professional is negotiating with a homemaker who has spent years raising a family on an allowance doled out by the income-producer. The spouse without such knowledge of the family's financial affairs or who is overpowered in arguments is most often the wife. She may have no idea of the value of the business or the practice, nor how much income it produces. She needs an attorney in mediation. It is not simply that she may agree to a settlement on terms more favorable to the husband; it is equally likely that she will make exaggerated demands in light of available funds that will render agreement impossible.

Dealing with Your Mediation Attorney

If you wish to be represented at mediation, you are perfectly justified in advising your attorney at the first meeting that you want to settle the case without court litigation if possible, and you want an offer extended to your spouse's attorney to mediate all issues. The attorney may have some requests of you that are quite reasonable. He or she may want you to acknowledge in writing that there has not been time to obtain all of the information about the extent of the marital estate that would be gathered in litigation or that the attorney would like to have. Or your attorney may ask for a delay in mediation until more information can be obtained or a consultant such as a CPA can be hired to evaluate data furnished to your attorney.

This latter request creates a dilemma for you. You want your attorney to be completely informed, but if both attorneys do the type of full investigation that would be done in litigation, not as much money will be saved by successful mediation.

You should probably permit a reasonable amount of investigation; but keep in mind that not all issues require investigation, and those that do not can proceed to mediation at once. Most important, you and your spouse can radically reduce the cost of investigation by promptly providing the other side with all documents or information requested or likely to be requested. If either side has to obtain court orders to get access to such things as check registers, canceled checks, bank statements, or business books and records, the cost will be enormous — and the suspicion engendered by the failure to be forthcoming may reduce your chances of reaching a mediated agreement.

You should be suspicious of the attorney who attempts to talk you out of mediation or has innumerable reasons why it will fail or why it is not an advantage to you. The bottom line is that a fair settlement agreement produced by mediation will save you money. This is the reason that mediation as an alternative form of dispute resolution has become so popular and becomes more so each year. This approach may not be the way your attorney is accustomed or likes to practice law. Indeed, the attorney running a divorce mill as defined in the previous chapter has no time or inclination to mediate.

Mediation will interrupt work on the case as it proceeds on the expensive conveyor belt of preparation for trial. If an attorney refuses to engage in mediation that you request, retain someone else.

Collaborative Lawyering, Another Alternative

A new concept appears to be gaining rapid acceptance in California. It is called *collaborative law,* and a number of attorneys throughout California have formed loose associations of collaborative lawyers. The idea came from attorneys in the Minneapolis–St. Paul area. Your author finds the concept the most exciting idea that has come to family law since income schedules fixing child support were adopted.

Here is how the process works:

Each party is represented by a capable attorney who is either a certified family law specialist or someone whose practice is substantially family law. The parties and their attorneys agree, preferably in writing, that they will make an exhaustive effort to settle the case without going to court for any purpose. Each agrees to quickly disclose all property and all information relevant to income without the need for discovery motions or depositions. Any request for information is to be complied with promptly and fully.

If there is a high earner and a low earner, the high earner, if needed, will agree to make funds for fees available to the low or nonearner's attorney, and agree to pay some amount of child and spousal support on an interim basis until full financial information is available.

Both sides agree that all evaluations will be done by an independent expert chosen by agreement. Neither attorney calls up a favorite "hired gun" appraiser or CPA. Each side willingly puts any representations it makes under penalty of perjury if requested to do so.

The negotiations will continue from day to day or week to week until the case settles on all issues or one or both attorneys conclude that they cannot settle the case in full.

If the case settles, a petition for dissolution, a judgment of dissolution, and an agreement are filed with the court after a judge signs the judgment. No appearance in court is required.

If the case fails to settle, each party is referred to a litigator who will commence to file motions, take depositions, send out interrogatories, retain whatever consultants are thought necessary, and do all of the things litigators do that make divorce so terribly expensive. The work will culminate in an agreement at a judicially supervised settlement conference, or worse, at a trial a week or so later. However, as the agreement to collaborate in an effort to settle provides, neither collaborative lawyer is eligible to represent the parties in litigation. Thus the failure to settle cannot benefit either attorney financially.

Pros and Cons of a Collaborative Law Approach

The advantages of such an approach as compared to litigation and mediation are the following:

1. It is obviously cheaper than litigation. There are no depositions of parties and experts and hence no preparation and review costs, no interrogatories to be prepared, answered, and reviewed, no court appearances for motions with attorneys and even experts sitting (and charging) for hours waiting for the case to be called, no special masters to be paid to oversee discovery or manage the litigation, and, of course, no trial preparation.

2. It is probably less expensive than mediation with attorneys involved because there is no mediator to pay. It is probably more expensive than mediation without attorneys, but affords the safeguards and security of having an attorney who can, among other things, insist that full disclosures, under oath, of all property be filed by each party along with the judgment. A failure to disclose all property will allow the judgment to be set aside and sanctions imposed on the dishonest party.

3. It is likely to be less time-consuming and emotionally draining for the parties. In mediation, the parties are almost always present for sessions that go on for hours. Attorneys feel the need to have the parties present to evaluate and accept or reject the recommendations of the mediator. In collaborative law, the attorneys can spend several hours coming to an agreement alone on several issues and then present it to the clients in a relaxed way at the attorney's office or on the telephone. Of course, if it is helpful, the clients can be present.

4. Even if the parties cannot settle all disputes, they may be able to reduce the issues to be litigated to one or two and thus reduce the cost of the litigation phase.

5. Because both attorneys are dedicated to settlement, they can approach the

divorce as a series of problems to be solved rather than as a contest. The disadvantages of collaborative law are obvious:

1. If the effort to settle without any litigation whatever fails, and few or no issues settle, then the parties must start with new attorneys who will spend many hours getting up to speed and pile litigation fees atop the collaborative lawyers' fees.

2. At various points in any type of court procedure, you may need someone to decide an intractable issue that the parties simply cannot agree upon. The pure collaborative process provides no such mechanism for decision, and one issue can impede the resolution of an entire case. However, some collaborative lawyers believe that the process is not compromised if the attorneys call a judge or respected practitioner to get an "advisory opinion" on an issue, even if they do not agree to allow the third party to make a ruling that is binding on the parties. Several years ago, two very fine attorneys were able to settle all issues with the exception of a very complex issue of property ownership. They called and asked me out to lunch, and over lunch they presented and argued the issue. I gave an informal opinion that they later conveyed to their clients and the case settled the following day. Obviously, if the collaborative lawyers start to seek rulings on every issue, they might as well be in full-blown litigation.

3. Some cases are just not appropriate for this process. One or both parties may be so focused on obtaining vindication or hurting the other party financially that they could never succeed in a collaborative process. It takes two to collaborate, and it may well be impossible to get your spouse to talk to an attorney willing to try this new process. Cases ripe for collaborative law are those where both parties go to a single attorney asking the attorney to represent both of them. Careful lawyers will not engage in such a conflict of interest, but they might well suggest referring one party to another attorney for a collaborative effort.

Your author will be watching collaborative law efforts to see if the concept becomes as popular with the family law bar as it appears to have become in Minnesota. I will be pleased to provide you with a means of contacting a collaborative lawyer if you will write to me c/o Impact Publishers, Inc., Post Office Box 6016, Atascadero, California

93423-6016, and enclose a stamped, self-addressed envelope. Collaborative lawyers for Southern California can be accessed on the Internet at www.nocourtdivorce.com. Collaborative lawyers for Nothern California are at WNW.nocourt.org.

DO'S AND DON'TS

Do...

- Consider mediation on all issues in your case before commencing litigation.

- Discuss with your attorney whether it would be advantageous to opt out of the public court system in favor of a private judge.

- Ask your mediator to inform both parties whenever a proposal is made that varies significantly from what the mediator feels would be the likely outcome in a court hearing.

- Consider a private mediator in a custody or visitation dispute if you are in a county that will not accord you confidentiality as to all aspects of the mediation.

- Remember collaborative law as a possible alternative to litigation and mediation if such a route seems feasible (especially if you and your about-to-be-ex are parting amiably).

Don't...

- Don't mediate the financial or property aspects of your case before anyone other than a retired judge with recent family law experience or an attorney with extensive family law experience.

- Don't mediate your case without representation by an attorney if you are poorly informed about the family's financial status or when you have been overwhelmed by your spouse in disagreements during the marriage.

P• Don't retain an attorney who refuses to assist you in obtaining a mediated settlement of the case.

• Don't assume that a private judge will cost more than remaining in the public court system, especially if cases in your county often do not go to trial on schedule.

4

Terminating a Marriage Without Financial Disaster

If you or your spouse choose to retain counsel rather than mediate dissolution issues first, or if mediation fails, you are in peril of spending up to three-fourths of your combined life savings on a dissolution. To avoid such a result, the case must be settled long before the pretrial settlement conference. Extended litigation with its ever-present depositions, motions, experts, conferences, and telephone calls will exact an unbelievably heavy financial toll, regardless of your wealth. Even if you can afford full-blown adversarial litigation, you didn't become wealthy spending money unnecessarily, so why do so now?

The High Cost of Litigation

How expensive is unrestrained litigation? Take as a given that a certified public accountant is seldom deposed in less than six hours. Thus, when your spouse's attorney takes the deposition of your CPA for six hours, each attorney's meter will be running at between $225 and $600 an hour and the CPA's will run at approximately $200 to $300. But each attorney does not come to the deposition without at least three hours of preparation, and the CPA is not about to subject himself to embarrassment when cross-examined. The CPA must spend at least three hours reviewing notes and calculating exactly what questions opposing counsel will ask and what answers will be most helpful to the client's case. The expert and attorney will spend an hour or more in face-to-face preparation for the deposition. So approximately 20 hours of attorney time and 10 hours of the expert's time will be spent on the deposition. Thus, the fees for the deposition of the CPA will be $4,500 to $12,000 for the attorneys and $2,000 to $3,500 for the CPA, and fees have not yet been considered for the court reporter or the time both attorneys and the expert must spend reviewing the deposition prior to a settlement conference. Reflect also that there is at least one other CPA to be deposed — your spouse's — and possibly two if the judge appoints the court's own CPA to resolve the dispute.

You and your spouse may be deposed for several hours, and it may be necessary to take the deposition of a real estate appraiser or an actuary, or both. Of course, all these depositions entail preparation and review time for attorneys and experts, both before attending the deposition itself and then prior to the settlement conference. Discovery alone, in a fairly routine case, can cost more than $50,000. And fees for time in court for various motions and preparations for these appearances have not been considered. I have assumed each motion, although taking no more than 20 minutes of actual time spent in presenting evidence, will consume 14 hours of attorney time, plus the time of any expert called to testify or be consulted, and will cost approximately $5,000 to $21,000 per motion.

Why Cases Fail to Settle

Cases fail to settle early for various reasons. One of these is that many attorneys never offer more in a settlement than their client's best possible case. They assume the judge will side with their client on each issue. It is not until the case is before a judge at a settlement conference — approximately a week or so before trial is scheduled — that such attorneys will drop this false optimism. As noted previously, courts seldom schedule settlement conferences earlier because it is not until people face imminent trial that they begin to negotiate seriously and abandon unreasonable positions. The reason for this intransigence is simple. The attorneys believe that judges at formal settlement conferences are apt to be more concerned with getting a settlement than doing justice. At the settlement conference, the judge is thus apt to ask each side what has previously been offered by way of settlement. The following scenario is common.

Assume you wish to purchase your spouse's interest in the family residence — a clear motive for wanting to keep the value low. The appraiser hired by your attorney puts the equity at $200,000. Your spouse's appraiser puts it at $250,000. The appraisers have predictably tilted toward their clients' interests. (They want to be hired again.) Your attorney hopes for settlement at a figure halfway between these two figures: $225,000. If your attorney, seeking a settlement prior to the settlement conference, offers to settle at $225,000 while your spouse's attorney stands on the $250,000 figure, your attorney believes that the settlement conference judge will suggest a compromise of approximately $237,500, halfway between the last offers by each side. By not making an earlier offer of $225,000, your attorney perceives that he or she has done you a favor by saving you $12,500. But I suspect you will pay three times that amount in attorney's fees for failing to achieve an early settlement.

For the same reasons, attorneys invariably refuse to make their best offers on issues of child and spousal support early in the litigation. If spousal support to be paid to you will be $1,500 a month if the court accepts *all* of your assumptions as to income, taxes, hardships, and overtime, and $1,000 if the court accepts *all* of your spouse's assumptions on the same issues, the tendency for each attorney is not to alter these figures prior to the settlement conference. Neither side will want to jeopardize a settlement at $1,250 that they believe a judge will recommend.

This approach not only will cost more in attorney fees, but it is based on false assumptions about how judges operate. To view settlement judges as doing no more than seeking to compromise all issues at a halfway position is a misconception of how a settlement conference works. Judges realize that if they simply choose a midpoint figure, the case will not settle unless both parties believe this figure is fair. Those who have settlement or family law experience will choose a figure that can be reasonably supported by income, county schedules, various hardships, earning capacity, and other significant factors. The recommendation is seldom a midpoint compromise. Often one party's best figure is accepted on one issue in exchange for the other party's best figure on another issue. But attorneys act in early negotiations as if such a midpoint recommendation is a virtual certainty.

Making a Better Offer

There are numerous ways your attorney can make a better offer without compromising your bargaining position should the matter later go to a settlement conference before a judge. Your attorney may suggest to your spouse's attorney that there may be some flexibility in your settlement offer if your spouse's offer is also flexible. Or better yet, an agreement (with specific penalties for violation) can be written, stating that neither side will mention to the judge any figures it offered in trying to close the gap between $1,000 and $1,500 in the support example mentioned above. But even if such an agreement is not possible, it is erroneous to expect the judge to simply choose a midpoint figure. In practicing law, I have seen innumerable judges look at a case and say, "Pay the demand. You're lucky it isn't more." If you allow the "midpoint myth" to control your bargaining tactics, the attorneys will do quite well financially. You won't.

Clearly the primary reason cases do not settle until the later stages of litigation is that the attorneys simply are too busy to pursue settlement. Even if you avoid a divorce-mill attorney and choose counsel who gives personal attention to your case at every litigation stage, you are not the attorney's only client.

A busy attorney will book extended hearings and settlement conferences at the rate of two or three a week far into the future. The nature of law practice is that each major event requires almost frantic preparation — often in the evenings and on weekends. Each hearing or conference will require the attorney's presence at the courthouse from half a day to a full day. When one case is resolved, another conference or hearing is bearing down on the busy practitioner.

Most attorneys have a system for the preparation of their cases, often with the help of an associate or paralegal, that will ready each case for hearing or conferences on schedule. Thus, it is unlikely your attorney will find time in the midst of preparing many cases to meet with your spouse's lawyer and seriously discuss settlement. As your case rides along the conveyor belt of preparation for the trial (that won't occur), through depositions, interrogatories, expert interviews, and motions, the meter is on for both you and your spouse; and your marital estate is dwindling.

Many attorneys see the scheduling of early and serious settlement conferences as an interference with the normal routine of preparing the case for litigation. Even if settlement efforts are built into the scheduling at your insistence, they are vulnerable to cancellation or postponement. When a crisis arises in one of your attorney's or your spouse's attorney's many other cases, the settlement conference is the easiest thing to scratch to free the attorney's time for handling the current problem. No judge is offended if a private settlement conference is canceled. The opposing counsel, having other crises to deal with, is glad to cancel the meeting and join in the illusion that it will be reset soon.

In reality, unless you have retained a flexible attorney with sufficient time and inclination to pursue settlement at regular intervals, your case will not settle early. Indeed, the first serious efforts to resolve differences will occur at the formal settlement conference set approximately a week before the case is scheduled for trial. And it will seem hard to fault an attorney who is carefully and competently marshaling facts and witnesses in preparing your case for trial.

One of the most competent and busy attorneys in Southern California is seldom available to receive or return telephone calls from opposing counsel, much less to discuss a settlement. She tells everyone who wants to discuss settlement, "My office manager has full authority to negotiate a settlement." Obviously, this is absurd. The office manager knows what the last offer was and what the client's goals are, but is not authorized to move beyond the last offer and toward a settlement. Such authority is not and should not be given to a layperson, or even a paralegal, but must come from a serious attorney-client meeting. This attorney settles many of her cases between settlement conference and trial. Her clients are *very* competently represented, but they do not realize the financial savings an early settlement brings.

Before hiring an attorney, you should commit him or her to at least three settlement conferences with your spouse's attorney prior to the settlement conference with the judge. The first should be shortly after you retain your attorney and before discovery has commenced. Your attorney may think it wise not to negotiate on issues that need investigating by way of discovery, but usually some issues can be resolved without any discovery. At this first settlement conference, the attorneys can set up a structure for future settlement of the case. They can agree to use independent neutral experts appointed by the court (more on this later); to provide — by a specified date — tax returns, business records, and bank statements without expensive formal discovery; and to send certain issues to arbitration. Although all issues cannot be settled, a message is conveyed to the other side that you are serious about an early settlement.

The second settlement conference should take place after the completion of a minimum amount of discovery and consultation with experts on the value of various properties. At this point, your attorney should put a serious offer on the table on every issue and demand that, if the offer is not acceptable to your spouse, he or she must indicate what *is* acceptable.

A third settlement conference should come when discovery is complete. If you have not already done so, you should now make your best offer as to every remaining issue, holding nothing back to await a conference with the judge.

When you hire an attorney, you should make it clear that the settlement conferences you want scheduled should be face-to-face meetings between attorneys, with you and your spouse nearby, available to comment on proposals. In some cases, it may be advisable to have the clients present in the room when the negotiations are under way. (Obviously both should attend or neither should attend.)

Settlement offers in letters are not nearly as effective. A settlement letter is usually the last correspondence to which busy attorneys respond, if they respond at all. Settlements are reached in face-to-face negotiations during which several counteroffers are made, and a perceived gain on one issue is balanced by a perceived loss on another. When letters are exchanged, neither such balancing of interests nor the making of confidentiality agreements that facilitate movement on an issue is possible.

Settlement Letters

There is another important reason why a written settlement offer may not be taken seriously. California law permits a judge to award sanctions (normally attorney fees that the other side is ordered to pay) against a party to a dissolution who fails to pursue settlement in good faith. Many attorneys, as part of trial preparation, send a monthly offer-of-settlement letter in an effort not to settle the case but to set up the other side for a later award of sanctions. Thus, the response is not a good-faith settlement offer but a "best possible position" offer intended only to avoid sanctions by giving the appearance of a genuine response to a settlement offer. Of course, the inept attorney ignores about four of these *pro forma* letters and the client ends up paying the other spouse's attorney fees as a sanction. Telephone contact is better than mail; but in my experience, attorneys serious about settlement meet face to face.

Cases fail to settle because clients don't provide their attorneys with data and information that is required before a settlement offer can be made or responded to, or data to which clients' spouses are legally entitled. The causes of this procrastination are many. Clients frozen by the emotional pain of the dissolution may find it easier to have a drink or a tranquilizer than to gather and review tax returns, canceled checks, and credit card statements.

Competent attorneys won't put up with this for a minute. They know that failure to produce data to which the other side is legally entitled, or that is required if they are to be prepared for hearing, is harmful to their image and reputation with the judge. Such attorneys will meet with the client, set a deadline for the production of data, and inform the client that they will withdraw from the case if the information or documents are not provided to them promptly.

Incompetent attorneys will let the matter slide until they are embarrassed in court and their clients are sanctioned by the judge. It is important to understand that the fees of such an incompetent attorney to his or her own client who is sanctioned will be higher in total than a good lawyer's charges to a client who produces the required papers when warned. That is why some terribly poor family law attorneys make a very comfortable living.

Finally, cases fail to settle because one side views a particular asset emotionally. There are spouses who refuse to permit the sale of the family residence, but insist they want it awarded to them even though they lack funds to purchase the house from their spouses and do not have sufficient income to make the mortgage payments. Or some parties refuse to buy out their spouse's interest in their pensions. This position is often motivated by a client's fear that after purchasing the spouse's share and beginning to receive the monthly pension after retirement, the spouse who was paid for his or her share of the pension will demand a portion of the income as spousal support. (The California courts have not supported the view that such a result is unfair, but the seller of the pension interest can agree not to "double dip" if this promotes settlement.) In other cases, both parties may be so attached to furniture or vehicles with little equity that they spend ten times what the goods are worth paying attorneys to haggle over them.

Using an Agreed-Upon Expert

To reduce the enormous cost of a dissolution, think of your strategy as two-pronged. The hiring of an attorney with an inclination to settle early is one prong; the other, equally important, is preparing for trial in a way that reduces expenses. You must never open the door to the hiring of three experts — yours, your spouse's, and the judge's — when one will do. Whether the expert opinion needed is that of a CPA, a child psychiatrist, or a realtor, your attorney should always propose that both sides agree on one impartial expert to resolve any issue.

When the parties agree on a single expert to make a recommendation to the court or to place a value on something, the cost of litigating the issue is reduced to one-third of what it would be if a battle of partisan experts ensued. If a deposition is needed, there is only one expert to depose, and only one expert to pay, rather than two or three. Agreement on a single expert also can pay a big dividend by enhancing the chances of settling an issue. A party is far more willing to accept the opinion of someone he or she has helped select than to accept the opinion of someone hired exclusively by his or her spouse. This is true even if the parties do not agree that the expert's opinion is binding. It is less likely that more than one expert will be needed if the negotiations begin with the appointment of mutually approved experts.

If neither party is unduly suspicious or seeking unfair advantage, finding an impartial CPA or real estate appraiser is not difficult. But intelligent dissolution litigants must avoid the "I-can-hire-a-better-lawyer-than-your-lawyer" nonsense, as well as the "my-expert-can-blow-away-any-other-expert" idea. Beware of the attorney who tells you, "I know an expert who can win this issue for us." The other side knows one too. Moreover, to agree on a neutral expert to be hired by both sides, each party must give up the idea that "if we agree on the right expert I can get an advantage." If both sides are trying to select a crony, they will never agree on an expert. Each party must be willing to agree to any person who has no direct or indirect ties to the spouse or the spouse's attorney, who has no philosophical or theoretical belief hostile to the party's view of the case, and who is perceived as fair and industrious by members of the local

Family Law Bar Association. Normally, experienced attorneys can agree on an expert whom each has previously hired and opposed. Even the most notorious "hired gun" among child custody experts or CPAs can render a fair opinion when engaged by both sides.

If the attorneys cannot agree, ask an experienced family law judge to name three experts he or she deems fair and knowledgeable. If the attorneys cannot agree on one of the three, then each side should exercise the right to reject one expert; the remaining unchallenged expert is then automatically chosen.

When an independent expert is selected, you and your spouse can either agree to accept that expert's opinion as final, or each of you can reserve the right to hire your own consultant if the neutral expert's opinion is unacceptable to either of you. The reservation of that right, however, is largely illusory. The settlement conference judge will presume that the opinion of the mutually selected expert is reasonable, unless you can point to some glaring error in the data on which the expert relied, or to some erroneous use of that data. This is highly unlikely.

The Litigious Spouse

You may be thinking that my advice is all well and good if your spouse and your spouse's attorney are cooperative, but what if they take an approach that will result in the waste of your family savings? What if they will not agree to neutral experts? What if your spouse has turned over the litigation entirely to counsel, will not suggest a settlement conference, and views the attorney as one who will mesmerize the court at a trial your spouse believes will occur? Your spouse is in such an emotional state that the loss of major assets presently is of no major concern. He or she won't read this book, and is told by the attorney that it is really only a formula for surrender, written by a judge whose motive is to reduce his workload.

In this situation, your attorney must continue to make settlement offers and to document each offer. Your attorney should also document failure to reply, or be prepared to show that the reply was calculated to promote litigation rather than to resolve differences. If a settlement conference is refused, your best settlement offer that can be made at the time should be put in a letter noting that the settlement conference was rejected. Ask for a written counterproposal if your offer is not acceptable to your spouse. In each letter, which can be sent as often as monthly, your attorney should ask for a meeting and ask opposing counsel to specify a convenient time. In this way, your attorney has carefully structured a scenario that should result in your spouse's paying much of your attorney fees. It is better to have your attorney's fees paid out of your spouse's half of the community property, or out of your spouse's separate property, than out of your half of the community property or your separate property.

If you are faced with an unreasonable spouse or a litigious attorney who will not agree to impartial experts, you will have to hire partisan experts. At this point, your choice is crucial to the outcome of any particular issue. Whether the expert is a CPA, a custody evaluator, or a vocational expert, only a small group in each field — likely not more than a handful in any given county — have scrupulously protected their reputation with local judges as objective and thoughtful seekers of truth rather than as partisans. These experts are known to the courts for their refusal to represent a litigant's extreme position when they cannot, in good conscience, support it. They are known to local judges as persons whose opinions are quite often accepted by both sides even when they have not been appointed as neutral experts. As soon as the opposing party's expert has rendered an opinion, this expert is quick to seek a meeting to resolve differences in an atmosphere of collegiality. This is the kind of expert you will want to retain; in custody cases, it is an absolute necessity. Such an expert may not fully accept your views or those of your attorney, but when you arrive at a settlement conference, you and your expert will have credibility with the judge.

I discuss expert selection in more detail in later chapters on substantive topics such as child custody and spousal support. Here, I simply want to stress that an expert who is a crony of your attorney, or whom your attorney has found "reliable" in the past, is unlikely to be the one who can best help your case. Your attorney should be aware of which experts are most often appointed by the judge as the court's witness, or whom your attorney recognizes as chosen regularly to appear with the judge on panels to discuss family law issues.[1] These are the people who can help your case.

Unfortunately, if your spouse refuses to agree to a mutually acceptable expert, it will cost you dearly; but for now, you are merely trying to cut your losses.

---

[1] Panels of family law specialists, including judges, lawyers, and various experts, are frequently presented as part of the continuing education programs established by the Family Law Bar.

Do's and Don'ts

Do ...

- Make a reasonable offer on every disputed issue.

- Instruct your attorney to enter into a written agreement with the other side that settlement offers will be confidential.

- Immediately provide your attorney with all data or information requested.

- Require your attorney to send you copies of all correspondence sent or received so you can make certain any settlement offer is promptly answered.

- Hire experts known to local judges for impartiality and objectivity.

Don't ...

- Don't allow the "midpoint myth" to control your attorney's settlement strategy.

- Don't permit your attorney to hire an expert without offering the other side the appointment of an independent expert agreed upon or appointed by the judge and paid by both parties.

- Don't hire an expert known to local judges as a "hired gun."

5
The Settlement Conference

If your case has not settled long before a formal settlement conference with a judge, the case already is a financial disaster for you, your spouse, and your children, if any. You have spent more money than the issues or the size of the estate could possibly justify. Here again, you are simply trying to cut your losses. Although you will find the settlement conference a difficult and uncomfortable process, your presence will be required, and it is certainly in your best interest to be present.

Judges view the settlement conference as the final step in settlement negotiations — a time to resolve the one or two issues still unresolved. If they find that the parties have not yet had settlement discussions or resolved a majority of the issues, most judges will be justifiably angry. A judge may take other actions that will not be in your best interest, such as canceling your previously set trial date and scheduling a later settlement conference. This can delay resolution of your dispute for up to a year, and will prove costly. If the judge can determine which party has been most culpable in failing to negotiate prior to the formal conference, the judge may impose money sanctions against that party.

If your attorney has failed to file a comprehensive settlement conference statement several days to two weeks earlier, outlining all issues and your position as to each, or has failed to attach the reports of all experts, you may be required personally to pay a money sanction to the other party, your settlement conference may be postponed, and you may be prohibited from calling the expert as a witness.

It is unfortunate that you can be forced to pay a sanction because of the neglect of an attorney. However, a Court of Appeals case holds that sanctions for frustrating the settlement of a case must be awarded against the client rather than the attorney, regardless of who is at fault. The client is evidently then to seek reimbursement from the attorney, in a malpractice action if necessary. The wisdom and fairness of the law continue to escape me. If the attorney is clearly at fault, it seems senseless to saddle the client with additional litigation.

In any event, California judges are quite serious about the timely filing of the settlement conference statement, not because it really assists the judge in the settlement of the case (most often, the judge has not had time to read the statements prior to the conference), but because the preparation of the statement requires each attorney to become conversant with the facts and issues of the case. It means the attorney has given thought to whether the settlement position included in the written statement will appear reasonable to the judge.

So you must insist that your attorney make every effort to meet face to face with your spouse's attorney in advance of the formal conference. If your attorney's offers to meet are rebuffed, they must, as noted earlier, be put in writing on a regular basis. Often the first question a judge will ask on a contested issue is "What have you offered, counsel?" It is important that your attorney be able to present a letter showing a concrete offer on that issue. If the question is met with a blank stare or with multiple excuses, let those come from your spouse's attorney. Moreover, the judge knows each attorney's reputation for settling or not settling cases reasonably. If your spouse's attorney, who is making the excuses, also has the reputation of being unable to settle cases early on, that attorney as well as your spouse may be on the defensive for the remainder of the conference, and you are likely to receive the benefit of the doubt on all disputed issues.

You must also be sure you are well informed on all issues before this conference takes place so you can make intelligent decisions yourself rather than relying entirely on your attorney. Ask your attorney to prepare a summary and the best possible result of each unresolved issue for you, as well as the best possible result for your spouse. Then ask what has been offered on your behalf regarding each issue, where your spouse stands on each, and what the cost would be to you if it became necessary to go to a contested trial. In this way, you can see how many dollars are at stake and what it will cost you to pursue them. Finally, if it appears that your attorney has offered little more in the settlement of an issue than your best possible result, insist that a better offer be made. This is also a viable strategy for settlement conferences that should be held long before this formal conference with the judge has even been scheduled.

If you have arrived at a late stage in the litigation without a settlement, and if you have documented both your reasonable efforts to settle the matter and your spouse's failure to respond reasonably or at all, then your attorney should insist on a hearing on attorney fees even if the judge settles all other issues. There is no reason to let an unreasonable or obstreperous spouse avoid monetary sanctions for frustrating a reasonable settlement of your case. Your attorney will need to be firm because the judge, having settled all issues and wanting to put the matter to rest, may suggest letting bygones be bygones. Your attorney must decline and explain that the case for sanctions can be orally presented in court in about 20 minutes or could be presented by written declarations presented by both sides to the judge for review.

Obviously, if your case should go to trial, your attorney will want to seek sanctions. (A sanction is an award of attorney fees or imposition of a penalty based on attorney or client misconduct rather than because one party needs assistance with attorney fees. In some instances, a finding of ability to pay a sanction may be a condition to its imposition.) This should be done in a hearing held after all contested issues have been ruled on by the judge.

DO'S AND DON'TS

Do...

- Evaluate each unresolved issue prior to the settlement conference in an effort to determine the best possible result for each side, where the settlement offers stand, and the cost of further litigation.

- Demand a hearing on sanctions for failure to settle if you are entitled to them. Insist on a hearing although all other issues have been resolved at the settlement conference.

Don't...

- Don't let your attorney attend the formal settlement conference without having previously made a realistic settlement offer on each unresolved issue.

PART

II

BASIC LAW AND
PROCEDURE

6

Shopping for a Judge

F orum shopping is the term judges and lawyers use to describe an attorney's efforts to maneuver a particular case in front of a judge the attorney believes will be friendly to the particular cause. Judges have reputations on many legal as well as social issues; for instance — to name but a few areas — whether they grant substantial or meager spousal support, whether they often or seldom follow recommended support schedules in setting temporary spousal support, whether they are willing or reluctant to order one side to pay for the other party's attorney fees early on, whether or not the award of attorney fees to the attorney for the low earner is normally reasonable compensation for the work done. More broadly, judges have reputations for gender bias; it might be said, for example, "She just doesn't like men," or, "He thinks every woman with children should be employed full time." A judge's orders on these issues are said to be "in the court's discretion," which means they will not likely be overturned on appeal. Thus, an attorney can greatly benefit a client's case by maneuvering it into a friendly atmosphere.

Judges, of course, are properly dedicated to preventing forum shopping. It is disruptive to the calendar and offends their notion that the result in a case is not significantly affected by a judge's biases or predispositions. In some counties, for an attorney to be accused by a judge of attempting "to do a forum shop" is akin to being accused of unethical conduct.

Some attorneys will deny that they forum shop. Others will privately admit that, of course, they forum shop; their duty is to do everything they can for their client including selection of an "appropriate" judge. I think most attorneys have preferences for given judges in certain cases and will attempt to guide the case before a "favorable" judge if it can be done without soiling the attorney's reputation at the courthouse as one who plays by the rules, and if it can be done without prejudicing the particular case for which the attorney is seeking a judge. The worst outcome is for you to be assigned to a judge who has become aware that your attorney has tried to get the case out of his or her courtroom.

Assigning Cases

The structure of Family Courts in various counties significantly affects an attorney's ability to forum shop; so does the method by which cases are assigned to a judge. Let us assume for a moment that the county is one with a defined Family Court in which several or (in the case of Los Angeles) many judges do work exclusively related to dissolutions, domestic violence, and custody and a few permutations of these. If the Family Court in that county uses the federal or direct calendaring method of assigning cases to judges, the opportunity for forum shopping is much reduced. Under such a system, dissolution cases are assigned by the clerk to judges in random selection when the case is filed. When the assignment is made, the judge hears all aspects of that case into the foreseeable future. The judge will hear all motions, preside at the settlement conference, and conduct a trial in those few cases that go to trial. Under this system, many attorneys consider it futile to go to trial because the judge has told everyone at the settlement conference essentially what he or she intends to do. Direct calendaring is now used in Alameda, Santa Clara, Ventura, and some parts of Los Angeles County, among other places. It is clearly the trend.

Under an authentic Family Court system using a direct calendaring method of assignment, forum shopping is almost impossible. I have heard of attorneys standing in line at the counter in the clerk's office and writing down what seemed to be the order of rotation and then attempting to put themselves in line when a given judge's name was up for the next assignment. I assume that if any clerk found such a practice to be prevalent, a random but equal selection of judges could be done by computer, as it is now in some counties.

Beyond standing in line, the only other way to obtain another judge is to use the one peremptory challenge given under California law to every party in the case. As discussed earlier, in California each party to a case has the absolute right to ask one judge to step down. The judge must do so if the motion is timely and proper. The party or attorney does not need to give a reason for challenging the judge, and the judge cannot inquire into the reason for the challenge. But the use of this peremptory challenge is risky. Your attorney, using the challenge, has no idea where you will be assigned; and the next assignment could be worse. Also, the assignment may not be random. In Santa Clara County, for several years, one judge was often challenged by defenders in criminal cases as being too tough a sentencer. The presiding judge's rule was to send any challenger of the tough sentencer to a judge whose policy was just as tough.

After a challenge, the presiding judge assigns the case to another judge. The presiding judge may know why you used the challenge and may counter by sending you to a judge in whom the qualities you sought to avoid are even more pronounced. Moreover, attorneys simply don't like to use such a challenge for fear that the judges will remember the event when the attorney is assigned there in future years. There is a saying among lawyers that once you challenge a judge, you must do so whenever assigned to that judge for the rest of your career. You can see why attorneys are reluctant to use this ultimate weapon; but as the client, you have the right to demand that such a challenge be used.

In a direct calendaring system, you probably can't even wait for the judge to go on vacation, because the clerk merely calendars matters before or after the ten or so days the judge is away. No other judge is likely to take the place of the vacationing judge.

The other method of assigning cases within Family Courts is the assignment method. Under such a system one or more judges hear pretrial or post-trial motions, one or two judges hear trials, and a third judge or two will hear long motions (normally in excess of 30 minutes but no more than one-half day) and also preside at settlement conferences. The judges may well shift their duties every few months with the judge hearing short motions moving to trials, and so on. The assignment system is ripe for forum shopping. By estimating a time for a motion that exceeds the limit for short motions, an attorney can bump the case to another judge. A short delay in filing a motion may produce a different judge after the judges change assignments. Determining when a trial or motion judge will be on vacation is very productive because another judge normally takes over the absent judge's calendar. Indeed, attorney "illness" or the need to be in another courtroom for 24 hours will usually result in another judge being assigned. The judge to whom you were or would be assigned is given another case rather than waiting for your attorney to recover or finish another case. If a case is assigned to one judge for trial, your attorney knows fairly well where the case will go if he or she can delay the start of the trial a day or so: to the other judge or judges hearing trials.

Assigning Judges

How experienced a judge are you apt to be assigned for a hearing or a trial? Not very is the answer, unless you are in Los Angeles County. Every rule has its exceptions, and a few judges genuinely like Family Court and volunteer for the assignment or agree to remain despite seniority that would allow them to leave. In most counties, however, family law assignments go to the least senior judges because those with greater seniority have taken the other slots.

Generally, the seniority system in San Francisco, Sacramento, Santa Clara and several other counties has placed Family Court in the hands of the least experienced judges. Worse, the assignment may go to a judge who resents being there or has no interest in family law — and it shows. Of course, the advantage of having a defined family law department of judges specializing in family law is that, although the judge may be new to judging, all of his or her experience is apt to have been in Family Court.

The exception to the rule that the least senior judges normally staff Family Court is, of course, the commissioners in many counties hired by the court to do nothing else for many years. And, interestingly, Los Angeles is a county where family law is one of the most popular assignments.

The reason it is popular in Los Angeles County is fascinating. The demand for "rent-a-judges" in Los Angeles County is very high. A rent-a-judge is a retired judge who sits by agreement of the parties and is given, for that case, all the powers of an active judge. Unlike an active judge, the retired judge is compensated by the parties at a rate of at least $325 per hour with no overhead attached. Thus, being rented is a very popular pastime for retired judges in the Los Angeles area, and retired judges are rented most for family law. Of all litigation where the parties legitimately need to put the case behind them and get on with their lives, the dissolution case stands first. The most rapid way one can get to trial is to rent a retired judge to hear the case. Since a high percentage of work for rented judges comes from dissolution litigants, senior judges in the last year or so before retirement opt for Family Court to add expertise in this area to their resumés — resumés rent-a-judge firms use to market the judge.

About thirteen years ago, when the first edition of this book went to press, San Diego County was a place where family law was a popular assignment. Prior to that time, San Diego had for too long been in the position of other counties: far too few judges for the caseload and a Family Court to which mostly junior judges were assigned. But twice in the 1980s, San Diego lobbied the Legislature for a host of new Superior Court positions. On each occasion, more than ten judges were appointed to fill the newly created positions. With each group of appointments, and especially the more recent group, the San Diego Family Law Bar, with the help of a few sitting judges, went to the governor's appointments secretary and sought the appointment of lawyers with a background in family law. They candidly expressed the view that family law judging takes a special temperament and a willingness to work in an increasingly complex area of law. I doubt anyone expressed the opinion that the judicial appointee with a prosecution background might not be enthusiastic and successful in a Family Court role, although that view is held by attorneys statewide.

The appointments secretary and the governor agreed, and as a result, by 1989 there were no less than seven Superior Court judges in San Diego County with extensive family law backgrounds obtained prior to their appointment to the bench; at least five of these were certified family law specialists. These judges enjoyed and sought family law work. Indeed, for a time, there were more judges seeking Family Court appointments than there were openings in Family Court. Moreover, this substantial group of dedicated judges with a sense of loyalty to family law had the influence to prevent the deterioration in working conditions for Family Court that had occurred in so many other counties. The San Diego Superior Court hired two full-time family law commissioners to assist with the workload. Counties of the size of San Diego at that time were fortunate to have one family law commissioner. The San Diego miracle should have been a beacon for the rest of the state, but unfortunately other county bar associations have not had the organization and audacity of San Diego's Bar.

Family Court deterioration is the experience in many counties where the bench as a whole looks at its new appointees and says, in effect, "Run this division as best you can with few judges and don't bother us." Some courts forget that the families of this state pay more taxes to help pay judge's salaries than out-of-state insurance companies and vendors.

Why Not Family Law?

There are a number of reasons most judges don't want a family law assignment. First, many are not equipped by background or temperament to tackle a new and complicated area of law where the judge must be as much a social worker as a judge. Frankly, good family law judges tend to be humanists.

Second, in most counties the assignment lacks prestige. "*Real* judges don't do family law," some judges say. This attitude stems partly from the advent of commissioners and the growing concept of family law as commissioners' work, not judges' work. Judges of prestige are thought to preside over death penalty cases and multimillion dollar injury or product liability cases.

Third, there are simply a number of judges who find the work personally distasteful, and that feeling should be respected.

Finally, I suspect many judges find the workload uncomfortable. In the last decade, Santa Clara County has averaged 9,000 family law filings per year and had only three judges to handle them. Each day brings the pressure of too many cases seeking courtrooms and no place to put them. Harried judges are desperate to obtain settlements, and the rest of the court is saying, "We would prefer *not* to see any of your cases in our departments."

Thus, if you find that your judge appears tired, a bit testy, and willing to approve *any* settlement terms so long as you settle, keep in mind you are seeing the results of a society that talks a lot about the importance of family and children but has seldom put its money behind either. You should also realize that this lack of resource allocation is why your case may have been assigned for trial to a judge who has heard no family law case in the past three years.

Do's and Don'ts

Do...

- Expect your attorney to know the biases and attitudes of local judges and you take his or her advice in avoiding certain judges.

Don't...

- Don't expect your attorney to hastily use a peremptory challenge against a judge.

- Don't insist on trying to avoid a given judge if you don't know who will ultimately hear your case.

- Don't expect the judge to whom your case is assigned to have much experience or seniority unless your judge is a family law commissioner.

7

Child Custody

An Overview: Who Really Makes the Decision?

Who is the most important participant in a child custody decision? The judge? The mother? Some stranger you've never met?

You may think it would be the judge, but I must ask you to reject that notion. Of course, the judge is the most important person in the sense that the ultimate decision requires the court's approval. But if one measures importance by relative input into that final decision, the judge's position is decidedly secondary in most California counties, and definitely in all major population centers.

Judges are certainly aware they are not well qualified by training or education to determine who should have primary responsibility for raising a child, and they have had little training in the art of interviewing children. Judges may have basic knowledge, such as knowing never to ask a child, "With whom would you prefer to live?" but some are uncomfortable in the role of interviewer. Moreover, the congestion in most California courts will not permit a judge to preside at a multi-day custody trial with formal courtroom testimony from parents, experts, teachers, day care providers, relatives, and friends. Such an approach not only is unnecessary to arriving at an informed decision, it would probably also hamper the search for what is in a child's best interests.

Thus, judges need qualified professionals to advise them on this most important of all decisions that Family Courts are empowered to make. Almost all California courts have established some system whereby a mental health professional is appointed to conduct out-of-court interviews and make a custody and/or visitation recommendation to the court. The judge follows the recommendation of the custody evaluator at least 86 percent of the time in permanent custody disputes, and 99.9 percent of the time in temporary awards of custody pending settlement or trial of the case. So it is this person — the custody evaluator — who possesses the real decision-making power and importance in custody matters, not the judge or the parents. If you don't understand that reality, it will harm your interests in the case. If your attorney doesn't understand it, he or she is truly incompetent.

Custody evaluators range in educational background from holders of doctorates in psychology to licensed clinical social workers. The extent of their education has very little to do with their ability. It ranges from persons with almost infallible judgment to persons with absolutely no judgment or common sense whatsoever; from persons with great insight into the needs of children to those with the capacity to make recommendations sure to harm them; and from those who know they must use investigation, judgment, insight, and perception in making a custody decision to a few incompetents who believe written psychological tests alone will lead to the correct result.

The structure established for the resolution of custody disputes varies from county to county. The evaluator assigned to resolve a custody dispute may be a court employee or a mental health professional in private practice who has agreed to accept court referrals at a reduced fee. Some counties use both court-employed evaluators and those in private practice. In several counties, the private evaluators may serve as backups to court employees who are unable to handle a burgeoning caseload.

When private evaluators are not the court's choice, but are foisted on the system as a result of court congestion, quality control becomes a major problem. The person may be on a list of those available for evaluation of custody disputes for no other reason than that the inability to establish a private clinical practice has led him or her to seek court referrals to supplement income. Often they have not undergone a complete interview, much less a rigorous evaluative process. Many private evaluators are well qualified, but persons unfit to do custody evaluations may go undiscovered for a long time. Attorney complaints are often thought to be nothing more than sour grapes due to a recommendation adverse to the attorney's client, and are thus not taken seriously by the court.

On the other hand, evaluators who are directly employed by the court or county are normally subject to a complete and competitive interview process. Selection errors are soon discovered because the evaluator's work is subject to ongoing scrutiny by a supervisor. I am not critical of private evaluators as a group. Several of the most competent evaluators I know are in private practice; but the ability levels within in this group are subject to wide variation. The fact is that no mental health professional capable of establishing a clinical practice and earning a decent living from it is apt to take great interest in consulting to attorneys and appearing at settlement conferences. Thus, private practitioners should not receive court referrals without being subject to an interview or evaluative process that seeks to determine whether they have the requisite judgment, skill, and insight for the task.

Mediation and Evaluation: You'd Better Know the Difference

California now requires the parties to a custody/visitation dispute to mediate their differences before the court makes more than a temporary award of custody or visitation. Thus, your first encounter with the public or private mental health professional will likely be in a court-ordered mediation. You will normally be assigned to the next name on the list, whether public or private. Of course, you and your spouse may agree on a private evaluator known to your attorneys to speed up the process and also provide the highest skill level available. To do this, you must normally be willing to pay the top dollar private mental health professionals receive; judges seldom refuse to accept a person mutually selected.

But during court referral to mediation, beware! In some counties (San Diego, Alameda, and San Mateo, for examples) you may not be in mediation at all. If your attorney is not sufficiently experienced to tell you the exact nature and pitfalls of the process in which you are about to engage, your position may be seriously compromised.

Mediation has traditionally been defined as an effort by an impartial third party to resolve a dispute between two or more parties by seeking to bring them to an agreement. It is not arbitration. No one renders a decision or a ruling. If mediation fails, it fails; and some other method or forum for dispute resolution may be employed, including resort to the courts.

State law requiring custody mediation does not define the term or establish rules for the process, so the nature of custody mediation varies from county to county. In counties that have a traditional form of mediation, the court-appointed mediator will involve you in a compromise process in which you and your spouse are encouraged to come to an agreement on one or a series of issues. What is said to the mediator by either party is confidential. If you fail to resolve your differences, you may be sent to an evaluator who will make a recommendation to the court or, in rare cases, you may go directly before a judge for a resolution of the issues. In this type of mediation, no one is intimidated into reaching an agreement. If parties reach an agreement through this process, because of its voluntary nature the agreement is not likely to unravel. The only coercion you might feel is your natural embarrassment if you should perceive that your spouse is making a genuine effort to compromise while your position is viewed by the mediator as somewhat rigid.

In other counties, custody mediation is quite different. After a few minutes of failed effort, the mediator will warn the parties that if they do not reach an agreement, the mediator will make a recommendation to the judge based on what has been said at mediation. This announcement is often followed by a statement that the judge almost always follows the mediator's recommendation (which is certainly true). If your attorney has not prepared you in advance, you may be shocked that the statements you have made may not be confidential. Indeed, every word you say is being judged by the mediator in order to advise the judge what the court should do. You may in fact *be quoted* to the judge. Moreover, if you say anything that offends the mediator, or take a position the mediator believes is unreasonable, the recommendation may be adverse to you. If not forewarned, you will suddenly realize that you are not in a traditional mediation process. You are in "muscle mediation" — "You-settle-this-or-I'll-tell-the-judge" mediation. You are actually in a form of arbitration in which, if you fail to reach an agreement, the arbitrator settles the matter by making a recommendation that is virtually always followed, as opposed to making an actual ruling as is expected in arbitration. Unless you know the ground rules in advance, you will feel that you would like to retract some of your prior statements to the mediator. If your spouse knew that you were engaged in muscle mediation and you were unaware of it, your spouse may have achieved a significant advantage.

The counties that use muscle mediation have a high percentage of settlements. Indeed, almost everything settles. No one doubts the efficiency of the program. Those of us who prefer the traditional mediation process, however, believe agreements reached at gunpoint unravel quickly. When one of the parties backs out of an agreement, the court is again clogged with the same litigation on the same issue.

There is an alternative to muscle mediation that is less crass on the surface, but still very coercive. If you inquire, the mediator will assure you that the mediation is confidential. You are told that if mediation fails, then the evaluation process starts. When mediation does in fact fail, you are given a later appointment to return for evaluation — whereby the evaluator makes a report and recommendation to the judge. But to your surprise, the appointment is with the person who acted as mediator — that is, the mediator and evaluator are the same. Certainly, you will recognize that while the statements you made in mediation were technically confidential, these statements undoubtedly will have influenced this person who now is acting as evaluator.

In fact, this evaluator may have already decided on a recommendation. You have been in a process only slightly less coercive than muscle mediation. Although the process formally has two steps, from the moment the mediation began you were also in evaluation. Again, if your spouse was aware of this and you were not, your case may have been irreparably damaged.

In the very worst form of muscle mediation, or same-person mediation and evaluation, judges permit evaluators to discuss the case privately with them before the parties and their attorneys arrive for the hearing at which the recommendation is to be made. This is absolutely illegal because it denies your attorney the right to cross-examine the evaluator on his or her opinions. Your attorney has the clear right to ask the evaluator under oath and on the record whether the evaluator has conferred privately with the judge. If the answer is yes and the court will not step aside and assign the matter to another judge, your attorney should seek a writ from the Court of Appeal if he or she believes the recommendation will be adverse to you.

Unlike traditional mediation, evaluation is a process during which the mental health professional forms an opinion on what custody and visitation orders would be in the child's best interests and recommends that order to the court. As noted above, if a court order follows the recommendations, then the evaluator's views must be stated under oath and subject to cross-examination. That is not to say that an evaluator cannot express an opinion to a settlement conference judge. But a court order does not follow a settlement conference unless the parties agree to the order; and, hopefully, the custody trial judge will be a person different from the settlement conference judge to whom the opinion was expressed without cross-examination.

Normally in-depth evaluations are made in preparation for a settlement conference and trial and take up to four months to complete. The evaluator not only may wish to talk to the parties together and separately several times, but also may wish to interview neighbors, teachers, and child care providers, among others. Of course, the evaluator also may wish to talk with the child.

Some counties have an emergency evaluation that precedes interim or temporary custody orders. The need for such an evaluation will occur when the parties cannot agree on a custody arrangement pending the settlement conference or trial, and one party alleges that the status quo pending settlement conference or trial represents a danger to the child's well-being. This emergency evaluation, called a *screening* in some counties, is accomplished immediately. A recommendation is made to the judge within hours and is usually adopted. But again, the expert opinion must be subject to at least brief cross-examination. In cases of alleged abuse or molestation, this emergency evaluation may take up to 48 hours to resolve if the police or juvenile authorities must be consulted.

Many attorneys believe a temporary placement order pending a complete evaluation often determines the entire case — that after a child has been with one parent temporarily for several months, the evaluator will conclude that the child should not be uprooted by a change in custody. This is simply not true. Innumerable times I have seen an evaluator decide initially that the status quo with one parent would promote a child's minimum safety or temporary well-being but, after a full evaluation, conclude the child would be better off with the other parent over the long run.

Custody: The Substantive Decision

Most experienced Family Court judges, if required to rank the factors that determine a custody award, will normally consider the most important to be the determination of "the parent with whom the child is most closely bonded or attached." To say that a child is bonded or attached to a parent is to say that the child feels safe, secure, and relaxed with that parent, and knows that the parent can be relied upon to meet the child's needs. This parent is not necessarily the parent who has spent the most time with the child, but there is a high correlation between the two.

The usual mudslinging that occurs in custody battles is often not very helpful to the slinger's case. Personal faults are not determinative of a custody dispute unless those faults have an effect on the person's ability to be a good parent. Obviously, if chronic alcoholism or drug use is placing a child in danger, such conduct may affect a judge's view of what is in the child's best interests. But even then, a judge may give the offending parent an opportunity to improve before prying a child loose from a parent to whom the child has strong emotional attachments. However, allegations of traits not directly related to the child — including charges of laziness, infidelity, untidiness, foul language, inability to provide much in the way of material goods, and even personality disorders — are normally a waste of time unless they can be shown to have a direct and detrimental effect on the child.

Moreover, a concentration on the other parent's faults tends to diminish the accuser in the eye of the evaluator. Even charges of drug abuse or alcoholism are two-edged swords. They are often hard to prove and, if unsubstantiated, will tarnish the accuser. Even if substantiated, although spouses may not abuse drugs or alcohol equally, seldom is the accusing spouse free of some taint, as the accused spouse is always quick to point out. As one fine family lawyer is fond of saying, "Divorcing parents, like dice, come in matched pairs."

Because the extent of bonding with each parent is so important in a custody battle, it seems puzzling that custody is so often in dispute. The parties normally know which parent has the strongest bond with the child. In the average case, the issue is rather easily determined by an outside observer. Rarely is a child equally bonded with both parents. If parents truly are acting in the child's best interests, they will acknowledge this. (Doing so requires no more than being honest with oneself and each other.) The parties should then agree to give the more strongly bonded parent primary physical custody of the child and accord the other parent frequent and substantial access to the child — often called "visitation" (in my view, a terribly destructive and unnecessary word).[1]

Often parents cannot sensibly agree on custody and access to a child because one or both have a hidden agenda. Hidden agendas come in all shapes and forms and never involve the child's best interests. For example, one parent wants to deprive the other of custody of a child as a punishment for perceived wrongs, such as an extramarital affair. Or one parent cannot bear the thought of the child's having affection toward the other parent's new mate. Or Dad wants more access to the child because his attorney has told him this will reduce what he must pay in child support (it will). What is common to all hidden agendas is that they meet the needs of the parent and not the child, who has become a pawn in an effort to achieve some advantage. In some cases, it is apparent that a hidden agenda exists; for example, where the parties haggle endlessly over who will provide transportation for a visitation period, or whether the plan of sharing will be called sole custody rather than primary or joint custody. (The child doesn't care.) In other cases, a hidden agenda is more difficult to discern immediately, but one or both parties have a concealed motive in the vast majority of custody and visitation disputes.

The better custody evaluators rely greatly on observation in reaching a conclusion. They focus mainly on the interaction between parent and child. Does the child appear relaxed or tense in the presence of a parent? Is the child hyperactive in the presence of one parent rather than the other? None of these observations can be conclusive. Of course, a child may express fear of a parent because of some untruth the other parent has told the child. But competent evaluators make judgments not simply on what they are told but also on what they see.

Obviously, a verbal history from both parents is important in determining past patterns of parenting, or the lack thereof, and the extent to which a parent has spent time with a child. But observation goes a long way in confirming or invalidating a parent's perceptions and resolving conflicts in the histories given by the parents. If

---

[1] The California Family Law Act has virtually eliminated the term "visitation" and replaced it with words such as "parenting responsibility."

Dad has spent as much time as he claims in nurturing the child, why does the child not seem to communicate with him at any level, but rather seeks Mom's attention or approval on most matters? Or why does Dad have so little confidence in giving directions to the child?

(A word of advice: *Always* refer to "our" child, not "my" child, during mediation or evaluation. The latter appears proprietary and implies the other parent is unimportant in the child's eyes.)

If you are a parent involved in a custody dispute, this information is very important to you. You will be aware that your interaction with the child is not merely subject to scrutiny in the evaluator's office, but may well be scrutinized in the courthouse corridors while you wait for your appointment.

If you believe your spouse might not play fair and would seek to "program" the child, giving your spouse custody of the child the night before the evaluation interview could pose risks for you and the child. On the other hand, efforts to alienate a young child from a parent for whom the child has genuine affection normally fail after the child is in the presence of that parent for even a relatively short time. During a span of 30 minutes to an hour, it is highly likely any "programming" will unravel. If one parent is using extraordinary yet covert efforts to control a child, a perceptive and insightful evaluator will pick that up by the second, if not the first interview.

Does the Child Have a Choice?

Judges are generally aware that children approximately 14 years of age or older cannot be required to live with a parent not of their choosing without creating some undesirable consequences for both parent and child. Unfortunately, this is true even if the child's choice for custodial parent is based on inappropriate or spurious reasons or motivations. The question most often posed by parents involved in a custody dispute over a child age 9 or older is "At what age will the court listen to the wishes of the child?" Often the word *listen* is used to mean *agree with* or *put major weight on* the child's wishes. My sense of current practice is that an evaluator or judge may be willing to listen to a child's expressed desires, or talk privately with a child as young as 8 years old. But depending on his or her maturity level, a child as old as 13 may or may not be "listened to" by the judge. So the real question is not whether a judge will listen to a child (most will), but rather how much weight will be given to the child's views.[2]   In California, the judge is required to give the child's preferences "due weight" — in other words, as much as seems appropriate in light of the child's maturity level, intelligence, and motivation for the preference. Thus, the judge has almost complete latitude.

Although age is one factor the judge will consider in determining the weight to give a child's expressed wishes, other factors he or she may consider are social maturity, intellectual maturity, depth of insight, degree of honesty, and the extent to which the views are those the child has arrived at over several years of experience. A judge is not interested in listening to the regurgitated biases of a parent who has influenced a child. A judge may well want a mental health professional to evaluate these factors before deciding what weight to give a preference expressed to the judge directly, or to the mental health professional.

There are several reasons why judges may occasionally have children meet with them in chambers. The judge may wish to evaluate a child's general feeling of well-being or attachment to a parent or, in some cases, a grandparent. This is not a terribly compelling reason to put a child through the stress, fear, and guilt often associated with the experience, if a comprehensive report from a mental health professional whose work the judge respects and whose opinions have been or will be open to cross-examination is available.

Another reason for an interview is that the child wants to tell the judge how he or she feels. A message may come to the judge (usually from a child over the age of 10) that the child has views about his or her best interests but is unable to find anyone who will listen. It is common for pre-teens and older children to feel trapped and that their views are being ignored. This is especially common when a child is not represented by independent legal counsel. After a judge interviews a child, the child feels less like a pawn and, whatever the result, has had input into the decision. It may also permit the court to explain to the child, either in chambers or in the decision, why the court has chosen not to follow the child's desires. This is important to the child's mental health and ability to accept the result.

A common reason for a child to talk privately with the judge is that the meeting is a compromise. Some crass and ill-informed attorney is insisting on the right to call the child as a formal witness in open court. The attorney believes the child will parrot the client's views, or will deny having told the mental health professional some fact that influenced the latter's opinion. The judge, rather than delaying the hearing or trial to appoint counsel for the child and unwilling to have the child put on the spot

---

[2] There is considerable evidence that evaluations and interviews are harmful to children, especially if they number more than one. A growing number of judges, myself included, take the position that they do not want to speak with a child unless the child can be helpful on a specific issue, or unless the child's views cannot be credibly attained in any other way. A judge may also decide to talk to a child if the judge is worried that the child may interpret a lack of access to a judge or evaluator as the discounting of the child's views by an impersonal system. In some situations, obtaining information from an attorney appointed to represent a child's best interests may be a much less intrusive way of getting the information.

in public, can effect a compromise by meeting privately with the child in chambers. The judge may occasionally be forced to have a reporter present and, in the worst case, the attorneys. If the judge allows the attorneys to question the child under oath in chambers, this is not much removed from the stress of testimony in open court in front of parents and relatives.

Judges are reluctant to have children testify in open court because children seldom want to be put in the position of having to take sides in a custody dispute. Granted, older children may indeed desire to express a view as to their best interests; but, more often, a child dreads the prospect of expressing an opinion. The child has either carefully avoided taking sides, or, as a means of survival, has secretly told each parent that he or she would be pleased to live with that parent. If testimony is now required, the child's carefully constructed balancing act is over. The child perceives that honest testimony will hurt and alienate one parent, and the stress on the child is extreme. Even an expressed wish to state an opinion to the judge may be nothing more than the child's effort to pacify the parent who believes the child's view matches his or her own.

The private meeting in chambers is always preferable to open-court testimony. In open court, the attorney calling the child to testify cannot wait to get to the ultimate question that the child so thoroughly dreads. But a skillful judge, perhaps aided by a mental health professional, can always determine a child's preference or non-preference without having to ask disturbing questions. Indeed, a meeting is often only a ploy to avoid testimony in open court, because the judge already knows the child's views, as reported by the evaluator.

A word of caution: Never promise that what a child says to the judge will remain confidential. Even the judge should be reluctant to promise a child confidentiality. This is a promise that often cannot be kept, and on finding the promise broken, the child feels a deep sense of hurt and betrayal. The betrayal is so vivid and at such a crucial point in the child's life that it may permanently affect the child's ability to trust others, especially adults.

Counsel for Children

The appointment of an attorney to represent a child is a tactic a judge may employ when one attorney insists on calling a child as a witness. An attorney experienced in representing children can prepare the child for the event, which helps lessen the shock of the ordeal. Most important, the threat to appoint an attorney to represent the child may accomplish a retreat by one parent from the stance that the child is an indispensable witness. Attorneys for children are expensive, and the judge can assess the entire fee from the party whose conduct has created the need for an attorney. Faced with the prospect of paying an additional $5,000 to $20,000, the parent insisting on the child's testimony may rapidly retreat from this position.

The practice of appointing counsel for children varies from county to county in California. The practice was begun in 1983 by The Honorable Leonard P. Edwards, a courageous judge in Santa Clara County who has dedicated his career to improving the plight of children caught in the legal system. His authority for such appointments was a statute passed in 1976 that had largely been ignored by judges and attorneys alike. The practice proved so helpful that other judges acted similarly. The statute was expanded in 1989 to set forth duties as well as rights of attorneys appointed to represent children.

Some counties have been swift to adopt this practice; others have not. In 1987, 1991, and 1992, as presiding judge of the Family Court in Santa Clara County, I appointed an attorney to represent a child about once a week on average. The professionals in Family Court Services, on learning of my willingness and authority to make such appointments, kept a steady flow of recommendations coming to my desk. My sense is that they saw an attorney for the child both as someone to advise the court on custody or allegations of molestation or abuse and as a strong anchor for the child to hang onto until the storm was over. Most important, the attorney could assure that the parents were following the court's orders. This is very important when neither party is represented by an attorney.

I recall a 1987 case in which a child showed many of the adverse symptoms of dissolution, including violent behavior. I appointed an attorney who spent a day with the child at an amusement park without charge, simply because the child needed an adult friend. I now appoint counsel for a child whenever I find the parents so caught up in the battle that they have lost sight of the child's best interests.

Although Santa Clara County has appointed numerous attorneys for children, my colleagues in other counties tell me that in their jurisdiction it is almost never done. Even the law providing statutory powers for such attorneys has not resulted in a significant number of appointments. I suspect that whether counties engage in the practice or not is solely determined by the views of the judges sitting in Family Court and the traditions established by prior Family Court judges. Once started, the practice may well be recommended and followed by succeeding judges over the years. If never started, inertia and ignorance tend to prevent its adoption. My sense is that some judges don't find the appointment of counsel for children very helpful, and others feel it is not good for the child because it might instill in the child an inappropriate sense of power in the litigation.

An accomplished family law specialist recently represented a child in a custody hearing before a Bay Area family law judge. The attorney confided that not only did the judge continually fail to ask him to cross-examine witnesses, but also the judge cut off his closing argument in five minutes, after hearing from counsel for the parents for more than an hour. The specialist had the distinct impression that the court considered him a nuisance.

A great deal of heat has been generated in arguments over whether the child's attorney is to represent the child's viewpoint or the attorney's view of what is in the child's best interest. Most judges want the attorney to represent the child's best interest as the attorney sees it, but also want to be informed when the attorney's view differs from that of the child. The reason for the debate is that the concept of an attorney taking a position contrary to the client's is almost unheard of in our legal system. This may account for the reluctance of some judges to appoint attorneys to represent children.

Whatever the local custom in appointing counsel for children, if you are involved in a custody dispute that is apt to be bitter, your attorney should know the practice of every judge before whom you might appear. This knowledge might well affect his or her strategy in presenting your case, and a failure to be informed might result in missed opportunities for you. If your child independently holds your views but is unable to get anyone's attention, it is certainly to your advantage to know whether the judge assigned to your case regularly appoints counsel for children.

Joint Custody

The concept of joint custody has produced much discussion and dispute in family law circles. Much of the rancor is a result of the failure to define the term. I intend to do so now so that the reader will not misunderstand my views.

Joint custody does not refer to, and need not involve, equal time-sharing, although many think the terms are synonymous. A court may award both parents joint custody of a child. Under such an arrangement, one parent may have custody during the week and on alternate weekends. The other parent may exercise the right to custody on alternate weekends and one midweek evening. That award is certainly not one of equal time-sharing, and yet it is phrased in joint custody language. Such phrasing has eliminated one of the most demeaning words in family law — *visitation*. Neither parent has been named the *visitor*.

Curiously, most of the criticism of joint custody is actually misdirected criticism of equal time-sharing. The error probably results from several factors. Obviously, it is a result of ignorance of the many ways California courts award custody. It also stems from the fact that some awards phrased in terms of joint custody do, in fact, involve equal time-sharing. That is, almost all awards of equal time-sharing are joint custody awards, but not all joint custody awards grant equal time-sharing. However, if one's experience with successful or (more likely) failed joint custody awards involves awards with equal time-sharing, one is apt to assume erroneously that the two are synonymous. Finally, because awards phrased in terms of joint custody normally involve a more equal sharing of time by both parents, those persons and groups who oppose this trend in the law find it appropriate and effective to attack joint custody as if it meant equal time-sharing.

The failure to define the concept is not a fault simply of lay people or even lawyers. Indeed, the California Legislature has used the term in statutes without defining it. Until recently, the statutes even created what some felt was a preference for joint custody, without explaining the concept. Although I cannot be certain, it appears the drafters of the legislation fell into the popular trap of believing all joint custody awards were equal time-sharing awards.

Custody evaluators sometimes use the phrase "joint physical custody" in a custody recommendation when, in reality, the time share percentage is 70%–30%, or even more disparate. This is often done to promote settlement, because neither parent wants to be labeled a visitor as the word "visitation" infers. However, each parent has a strong stake in how the parenting plan is labeled. That is because a parent with "sole custody or primary physical custody" has the almost unfettered right to remove the child to another state or across the country without the other parent's consent. Therefore, a father who consents to his children's parenting plan being labeled "sole custody" to the mother, or who grants to the mother custody greater than 55% of the time, is at risk of losing his children to a relocation by the mother. The mother who agrees to a "joint custody" plan to pacify Dad may be making her and the children's further relocation more difficult. (See later in chapter the effects of time sharing on relocation). Note that a designation of "joint *legal* custody" has no such effect on relocation rights.

Equal Time-Sharing

Having eliminated joint custody as an issue, I can more cogently discuss the real source of controversy — *equal time-sharing*. Since sole physical custody has traditionally been awarded to mothers, the impetus for equal time-sharing has come mostly from fathers' rights groups, while most women's groups have been hostile to the concept.

Equal time-sharing began as a fad several years ago. As with fads in medicine, no solid data supported it; no research acceptable in a good department of sociology or psychology or child development existed to suggest equal time-sharing, as opposed to the need for contact with both parents, benefited children generally. Nor was there any contrary evidence.

If equal time-sharing has been overused, in my view it is the result of mediation. Recall that in California custody disputes must be mediated before being presented for judicial decision. This mediation occurs before overworked and harassed mental health professionals who need a high percentage of the parties to reach agreement if they are to avoid impossible levels of stress from overwork. A suggestion of equal time-sharing is an obvious vehicle to reach an agreement. It seems so fair and equitable that both parties fear that refusing such a proposal will make them look selfish. The pressure to accept the suggestion is much greater in counties practicing muscle mediation, where the parties fear the mediator will paint them in a bad light in front of the judge. Thus, the overuse, or at least the apparent popularity, of equal time-sharing came as a result of its value as a useful mediation tool rather than actual judicial decisions.

Whether or not equal time-sharing is in a given child's best interest is a separate question. My sense is that equal time-sharing mediation settlements did not focus on that question in sufficient depth, if at all. More recently, equal time-sharing has fallen into disfavor or at least less favor with the courts for reasons probably about as compelling as those that produced its favor. It is hard to tell whether this decline in popularity is related to a concerted attack by women's groups or some recent research suggesting this arrangement may, in some instances, lack the beneficial aspects for which it was originally credited. I suspect a little of both is involved.

Equal time-sharing is normally too cumbersome to be initiated or continued once a child reaches school age, although I am aware of a few instances where the parties live in close proximity, so where the children go after school depends on which parent has custody for that night. Whether this arrangement benefits the children or whether they are caught up in a daily struggle of wills between parents, I have no idea. The opposition to such plans, as with most equal time-sharing, claims that such arrangements are too confusing to the children — as if they can't remember or need to be reminded where they are to go after school. Another favorite criticism heard from the attorney whose client opposes equal time or merely equitable sharing of time with a child is that it involves too many exchanges of the child and therefore is somehow disrupting or confusing. Of course, there is no reason whatsoever that equal or more equitable time-sharing necessarily involves more exchanges than traditional visitation programs.

Before a child reaches school age, equal time-sharing is a viable alternative in certain situations. Many judges will consider an equal time-sharing award if both parents have nurtured and cared for the child since birth and the child appears to have a psychological bond with each parent so he or she will not be made anxious by being away from one parent for several days at a time. In my view, it is not often that a child is equally or almost equally bonded with both parents, so equal time-sharing is indicated only in a minority of instances.

Even if a child is strongly bonded to two active caretakers, most judges avoid equal time-sharing if bickering, hostility, and tension exist between the parents. It is generally thought that equal time-sharing will exacerbate the situation, or increase the child's exposure to an unhealthy situation. Knowing that judges hold this view, one party might be encouraged to act in an uncommunicative or obstreperous manner in an effort to kill an equal time-sharing award. Unfortunately, such a tactic is sometimes effective. If the ploy is used, it may well be the tactic of Mom, who believes if the judge is forced to reject equal time-sharing, a traditional gender bias of courts in favor of mothers as the primary custodians will result in an award of primary custody to her. Thus, it is extremely important that a judge cultivate a reputation for being free from gender bias in custody situations. As discussed earlier, not only does gender bias result in forum shopping by attorneys but it can also encourage conduct adverse to a child's best interests.

Judges need legislative support in eliminating inappropriate conduct as a ploy to defeat equal time-sharing. In 1987, the California State Senate was considering a bill that would have removed from the Family Law Act the concept that the ability to share a child is a mark of good parenting and a factor to be considered by the judge when awarding custody. Santa Clara County judges actively opposed the bill and encouraged other judges to withhold support until the provision was restored to the bill. Our success allows a judge to let both parents know early on that a demonstrated lack of ability to share could cost the offender primary custody of a child. The statute, as it presently reads, encourages custody evaluators to make recommendations adverse to a parent with demonstrated lack of ability to share a child. Anyone involved in custody litigation should be forewarned. A selfish attitude toward the other parent's access to the child can result in the judge's refusal to award primary custody to a parent who would otherwise be preferred under other standards of good parenting.

The bottom line on equal time-sharing is that judges vary in their receptiveness to the concept. Older judges tend to be less receptive than younger ones. Judges with strongly fundamentalist religious views are less open to the concept than other judges. Mom's historical relegation to the home has had the side benefit of causing her to be viewed as the more appropriate provider of child care.

It is important for a person involved in custody litigation to know that judges who hear custody disputes have reputations for openness to or rejection of the concept of equal time-sharing as a viable option. Your attorney should know the reputation of each Family Court judge in this regard and be willing to use efforts to maneuver your case in front of a judge with views helpful to your position. Again, the selection of counsel is all-important. Only a local attorney with several years experience can be expected to know the views of each judge on this issue, and the subtle differences between seemingly similar views of two judges. An attorney's knowledge of the views and biases of a judge who could potentially preside over your settlement conference is certainly more important than pure forensic skill. (Remember, your case is probably not going to trial.)

One major qualification should be mentioned. If your case is to be litigated in a county where you are likely to be assigned for settlement conference or trial to a judge who may have had little background in family law, then your attorney cannot be expected to have knowledge of the judge's attitude on specific family law issues. But even in that situation, your attorney is not entirely helpless. Civil or criminal lawyers who have had extensive experience in judges' courtrooms and are aware of their values can provide important information from which one ought to be able to make an educated guess on each judge's view of equal time-sharing, joint custody, spousal support, and a host of other issues.

One final note may be helpful to someone seeking or opposing equal time-sharing. A child's day care provider or teacher can normally be expected to oppose equal time-sharing. Generally, teachers and child care providers have an inordinate hostility to what they call joint custody but which is, in fact, equal time-sharing. Although some might suggest this stems from laziness — that teachers and child care providers are weary of keeping two persons informed of a child's progress or well-being — this is very doubtful. The more likely explanation is that the only time a child care provider or teacher becomes fully cognizant of a joint custody arrangement is when trouble develops. A child care provider may know parents are sharing time with a child more or less equally, but the strong awareness that molds one's views on the subject comes when the arrangement is not working well and the teacher or child care provider is drawn into the fury. It is perfectly understandable that one whose only real association with a concept has come in unpleasant circumstances will not be likely to support the concept.

Move-Away (Relocation) Cases: 180-Degree Changes — Twice!

Prior to 1991, most Family Court judges assumed that the primary custodial parent could move with the child anyplace in the world that parent wished to live and the noncustodial parent was helpless to prevent the relocation of the child. To do so, the noncustodial parent was required to prove that the move was detrimental to the child — a burden of proof that can seldom be met. Then, in 1991, a California Appellate Court, in *In Re Marriage of Carlson* said that the assumption was wrong. A child could be moved by a custodial parent only if it was in the child's best interests; the party wishing to move had the burden of proof on the issue. Moreover, the parent wishing to relocate a child had to prove the move was necessary, rather than merely convenient. *Carlson* was an affirmation of Family Code Section 3020, which states that it is the public policy of this state to assure minor children frequent and continuing contact with both parents, after the parents have separated or dissolved their marriage.

A short time later, another California Appellate Court held that the first duty of a trial judge is to restrain the move until a full and complete hearing and investigation could be held. As a result of these appellate cases, the ability to relocate a child was severely limited by California trial courts. When these courts asked whether it was in the best interest of the child to move to another area with one parent, or to remain in the area where the child could have frequent and continuing contact with both parents, relocation was seldom found to be in the child's best interest.

Several more cases followed this line of thinking until five years later, in 1996, the California Supreme Court decided the case of *In Re Marriage of Burgess* and again turned the law on its head. According to *Burgess, Carlson* and its many progeny were wrongly decided. The custodial parent need not prove the move was necessary. Moreover, the burden was on the noncustodial parent to prove that the move was so detrimental to the child that an immediate change of custody was required to protect the health and welfare of the child. That burden was almost impossible to meet. Perhaps if the child had an illness for which care was available only in the local area or was a teenager demanding to stay in the same school with longtime friends rather than relocate, a trial court might find that the move was detrimental to the child. But those situations are unusual. The relocating parent had only to show that the move was not for the purpose of denying the other parent access to the child. That is, that the relocating parent was acting in good faith.

It is now almost impossible for the noncustodial parent to prevent a relocation of the child. Since the mother is most often the custodial parent wishing to relocate, women's and mother's groups were overjoyed and father's rights groups were in a state of shock. The *Burgess* case rejects the notion that a child obtains stability from having two active parents. Instead, *Burgess* stands for the proposition that a child obtains stability from the primary custodial parent, and the bond with that parent is not to be easily broken.

The reason that *Burgess* has generated so much litigation is what the Supreme Court said in footnote 12, almost as an afterthought. If the parenting plan was not that of a primary parent but, instead, was joint custody, then a new trial was necessary on the issue of custody and the test was then the "best interests" of the child. Under those circumstances, it would be much more difficult to relocate a child. As a result, some fathers are no longer willing to agree that the mother will be the primary custodial parent, but are demanding that the plan be one of joint or shared custody out of fear that if they agree to the mother as the primary custodial parent, the child will be on the East Coast the following year. We do not know how much time a parent must have with a child in order for the parenting plan to be deemed one of joint or shared custody. California appellate courts have held in two different cases that if a father has the child approximately 36% to 38% of the time, that is *not* joint custody. It would appear that for the appellate courts to find that one has a significant amount of time with a child (the test for joint custody), it must be more than 40 percent. How much more is anybody's guess at this point.

Move-away cases are themselves highly litigated. The nonrelocating parent sees the relocation as tantamount to the loss of a child. Thus, that parent seeks to establish that the move is in bad faith; that is, it is calculated to deprive that parent of access to the child. This approach may prove very successful if the parent wishing to relocate has a history of frustrating visitation and the move does not seem to be based upon a good reason.

Many custody evaluators are hostile to *Burgess*, because it requires them to ignore a child's best interests time and again. They may also hold the view that it marginalizes the role of fathers in a child's life. Thus the evaluator may ask, "If the move is not necessary, why does the custodial parent wish to move?" From there the evaluator may conclude that the purpose is to deny the noncustodial parent access to the child, especially if there has been a history such conduct. If the trial court finds the mother (the usual custodial parent) in bad faith, the move will be disallowed and custody will be changed if the parent wishing to move in fact does so.

One further word of caution: Do not ever relocate a child without court permission or the written consent of the other parent. Although you may ultimately be given the court's permission to relocate the child, a unilateral move may result in the court ordering the child returned to California until a complete investigation and hearing can be held. Indeed, your relocation can be seen as a child abduction and result in a loss of primary custody. At the least it will cause the evaluator and the court concern about your judgment as a parent.

Choosing an Evaluator

In Chapter 4, I discussed the selection of an expert witness for financial issues. The selection of an expert for custody litigation is so vital to the outcome of the case that I want to give particular attention to the privately retained custody evaluator. But the advice I gave as to the selection of experts in general applies equally to experts in custody cases.

In California, the mental health professional who will serve as a custody evaluator is either appointed by the court or is someone both parents have agreed to use as an independent expert. Undoubtedly, the only time you will face the issue of hiring a privately paid forensic expert is when you learn that the opinion of the court-appointed or agreed-upon expert is adverse to you either relating to primary custody or visitation rights. Regardless of which one, let us assume you believe, for the sake of your child's well-being, you simply cannot live with the result that will be recommended to the court.

At this point, I would encourage you to reflect for a day or so before instructing your attorney to hire a mental health professional in an effort to obtain testimony that is contrary to the opinion of the court-appointed expert. At this stage, your chance of gaining primary custody over the recommendation of a witness appointed by the court is no more than 15 percent. If the dispute is over visitation, your chance of prevailing may be slightly better.

Judges are loath to rule against a court-appointed evaluator. They appoint evaluators in an effort to settle cases. A judge who rejects the opinion of an appointed expert knows this sends a message to the bar that further litigation after the independent evaluator's opinion has been made public may be successful and is worth the effort. Such a message does not promote settlement.

I do not for a moment wish to be interpreted as suggesting a judge would ever rule against what he perceived as the child's best interests simply to promote settlement in other cases. What I mean is that the judge's desire to settle litigation creates a strong presumption of the correctness of the independent evaluator — a presumption difficult to overcome. Since the case is already a financial disaster for you and will become more so, a short period of reflection before you commit to an objective that is improbable demonstrates wisdom and maturity. A relatively long "where are we now" conference with your attorney is strongly recommended during this period.

Your choice is not simply to surrender or to hire your own expert. Your attorney may be able to negotiate a settlement someplace between the expert's opinion and your position. I admit that dissemination of an independent opinion in favor of one party often causes that party to "smell victory" and resist any modification of the recommendation. But that party is bound to be hurting financially, too, and may even face the prospect of paying a portion of your attorney fees and expert costs. Thus, it may be worth a try.

In addition, I think there are some questions you need to ask of yourself and your attorney. Indeed, you may wish to seek the advice of another attorney or a mental health professional in answering them.

1. Is the opinion of the court's witness obviously flawed?
2. Can you point to misinformation on which the witness relied, or conclusions that clearly do not follow from the data?
3. Do you have more than a general disagreement with the conclusions?
4. If you can point to specific errors, are they demonstrable to a judge?

Errors you have spotted are not helpful unless they will also be obvious to an independent observer conversant with the case. If you seek a second opinion from a mental health professional, withhold permission to interview the child. As discussed earlier, multiple interviews may harm a child's mental health.

If you have your own therapist, by all means discuss the effects of further litigation on you and your relationship with your child. If you do consult another person, you must make it clear that the person whose advice you seek will not be hired as your attorney or your consultant. It is essential that you remove any possible economic motivation to recommend litigation from the persons whose advice you seek.

If after reflection you are convinced the independent evaluator's opinion is based on demonstrably flawed views or perceptions, then you, with the help of your attorney, must choose a mental health professional who will try to convince the judge of the merits of your position. It is essential that you not let your attorney hire an expert with impeccable credentials but a reputation among local attorneys of supporting the position of the hiring party. If you follow that path, your case is lost. Whatever reputation that mental health professional has with local attorneys also exists with local judges. A "hired gun" witness will have no credibility with the settlement conference judge. (Of course, such witnesses may be credible to judges without family law experience, unless they have testified so often in so many different ways that the local Family Law Bar has a "book" on them that can be used to embarrass them in front of any judge.)

Resist the temptation to hire only an expert who will agree with you. Instruct your attorney to find an expert who is known among local attorneys and judges for refusing to testify in cases where the expert does not agree with the position of the party paying the witness's fee. There is, of course, a risk in hiring such an expert. He or she may decline to support your case after billing you for interviewing people and gathering data. On the other hand, if such an expert agrees with your view, your chance of overcoming the independent expert's opinion, while still less than 50 percent, will be immeasurably enhanced.

The characteristics of the forensic mental health professional whom I recommend can easily be described. Obviously, you want someone who has scrupulously protected a reputation for objectivity with local judges. You need an expert who is known for refusing to become involved in litigation as a partisan. Avoid the expert who testifies as a witness hired by one side only, as opposed to being court-appointed or agreed to by both sides. The professional's forensic experience should be almost exclusively as a result of court appointments or as an agreed-upon expert.

Forced to choose between a mental health professional with almost no forensic experience and a "hired gun" with a resume (and reputation) stretching half the length of the courtroom, I would choose the former. If you must hire an expert who has testified as a partisan witness on a *few* prior occasions, look for one who has never made a custody recommendation before a judge without having interviewed both parents and the child; although not uncommon, nothing is more destructive of an expert's credibility in the eyes of a judge, and judges do chat with one another about expert testimony in their courtrooms.

The ideal expert is someone who may have made major financial sacrifices both to benefit innocent children and to maintain a spotless reputation with the courts. The person might be a recently retired evaluator from the court's staff of mental health professionals who has *not* gone into private practice to do court-related work, but into clinical therapy or research. He or she might be someone who has little Family Court experience, but who is often appointed by the judge in Juvenile Court dependency cases. (These are cases where children may be removed from the custody of a parent for a variety of reasons, including physical, sexual or emotional abuse, neglect, or exploitation.) The expert might be an academician who seldom gets involved in litigation but is willing to help in an extraordinary case.

If you are able to find an expert known to local judges as one who puts the needs of children ahead of the litigation, the arrival of that person at a settlement conference or trial will signal the judge that something might be amiss in the opinion of the court-appointed witness. Even if the person is unknown to the court, not having a reputation as a "hired gun" is a distinct advantage.

What if you hire an expert and, after gathering and evaluating the data, he or she declines to support your position? If your concern is for your child's best interests rather than your own needs, seriously consider ending the litigation. An independent expert and your own expert have agreed with the other parent. Perhaps they are correct. You can still hire another evaluator, but you won't win; and further litigation and turmoil may do lasting psychological damage to your child. The child has already been interviewed by at least two experts. Do you want to add another, and perhaps a settlement judge?

If you are faced with the adverse opinion of a court-appointed or agreed-upon witness, there is one final tactic open to you that meets the needs of you, your child, and the judge. You want an expert to review the opinion of the court-appointed or agreed-upon witness. Your child needs to avoid the rancor, tension, and pain that go with a trial. The judge wants the case settled. Your attorney might approach the judge in the presence of opposing counsel and suggest this scenario: The judge will appoint a second expert with the authority such an appointment bears. The other parent and the child will be available for interviews. The expert, if possible, will be agreed upon by both parents. You will pay the fee of this second court appointee. The second expert will not be permitted to see the written report of the first. If the custody recommendation is the same as that of the first expert, you will agree that the opinion of either may become the order of the court.

As a family law judge, I have granted a number of such requests. The suggestion certainly meets my needs. Since *independent* mental health professionals normally agree in their recommendations, the opinion of the second expert will probably be the same as that of the first, and the case will settle. If the second opinion differs, I am alerted that the case is a difficult one and a child's well-being may be in danger. As a recipient of an adverse opinion from the first expert, you can use this approach to obtain the opinion of another expert with all the credentials and credibility of the first. The second expert will not come to the settlement conference as a partisan advocate. Moreover, the mere appointment of a second expert may make the other parent more amenable to a settlement. Your child will avoid a trial if the case settles, and if it doesn't, the child may ultimately benefit from the second expert's opinion. Finally, your spouse may benefit by avoiding the expense of a settlement conference or trial and paying nothing for the second opinion.

Whether the judge will grant such a request will depend on your attorney's ability to convey the idea that this is not an ordinary disagreement with the opinion of the court-appointed expert, but that certain factors make that opinion far more suspect than usual. Of course, the granting or refusal of the request also depends on the judge's flexibility or philosophy, as well as the extent to which local court rules weigh against such an appointment.

This approach has one often overlooked advantage: You avoid the pitfalls of employing your own expert. If you hire your own expert to rebut the opinion of the court's expert, your expert may have difficulty obtaining an interview with the other parent and with the child. Having an initially favorable recommendation from an independent witness, your spouse may refuse to submit to an additional evaluation. Your spouse may also refuse to submit the child to further interviews, citing reasons suggesting that multiple interviews harm a child's mental health. Although your spouse's effort to avoid another evaluation will probably fail, I am not certain how a given judge might rule with reference to the child. Fearful of an adverse ruling, you may use a visitation period to sneak the child off to your chosen expert. But if you do not have primary custody, everyone including the expert will be embarrassed when he or she is asked by whose authority the child was put through another interrogation. Agreement on a court-appointed second expert avoids these snares.

The Molestation Charge

Family Courts nationwide are feeling the effects of a new fad being used by parties to a custody dispute — the charge that the other parent is molesting the child. If the allegation is true, a parent is under a moral and legal duty to make the charge. If it is not true, there is no more reprehensible act. That is not changed by the fact that you *believed* the molestation occurred, unless some reasonable objective evidence supports the allegation.

The impact of such an allegation on the custody litigation is swift and major. County officials (often called Child Protective Services) undertake an investigation. The Family Court judge is apt to cut off the accused's access to the child pending completion of the investigation. The child is subjected to repeated evaluations (I have seen one case with more than 20) by police officers, social workers, medical doctors, mental health professionals already involved in the case, and court staff evaluators. The long-term psychological damage is certain. The child may be denied access to a loving and supportive parent for weeks or months. The officials charged with investigating the matter give it low priority. Why? The judge has suspended the visitation or custody rights of the accused parent, so the child is no longer in danger. Law enforcement and county officials seldom see long-term denial of access to a parent as terribly harmful to a child.

If the charge is true, the child is obviously well served. But unlike molestation charges generally, those made against a parent during a custody battle or dissolution are often untrue. They are the neurotic response of a litigant filled with rage and hate for the other parent. Although I have no statistics, my sense is that less than 50 percent of the allegations against a natural parent in the context of a dissolution appear to be true. The percentages resulting in criminal charges are less, and provable charges still less. Allegations against a stepparent or a natural parent's new mate or a relative have a far higher percentage of reliability and prove credible in a majority of cases, even in the dissolution context.

Judges are continually frustrated by the ploy of alleging a molestation to obtain an advantage in custody proceedings. It is a monumental task to find a mental health professional with the courage to clearly support or refute it. Typical reports conclude with words to the effect, "I can't say for certain that a molestation occurred, but some event happened to put the child in turmoil and fear of his father." (How about continual warnings and influences by Mom that Dad intends to do something bad to the child, or already has?) The cases drag on forever, and the wrongly accused parent loses all confidence in the legal system. Whenever possible, if a parent has knowingly and falsely alleged molestation, a judge will order her or him to pay all the other party's attorney fees and may well deny the charging party custody of, or access to, the child. Unfortunately, the evidence is seldom clear enough to permit such an award. It is usually impossible to determine that the accuser had no good-faith belief in the charge. Who can say for certain what a child may or may not have said privately to the accuser? Sadly, in the throes of a dissolution one parent is willing to believe things about the other that would have sparked an indignant denial at a happier time in the marriage.

If during dissolution you are wrongly accused of molesting or abusing your child, you don't have many weapons at your disposal, but you can do a few things to improve your position. Insist that your attorney immediately ask the judge to appoint an attorney to represent your child. The primary duty of the attorney should be to press authorities to conclude their investigation with something other than "the charges were not substantiated" or, worse, "were not provable." The attorney for the child can also form opinions on the molestation issue, but probably should not be permitted to interrogate the child concerning the charge. The attorney would just be another in a long line of evaluators, and the least qualified by training and background to render an opinion.

You should cooperate fully with the investigation of the police and social service agencies. Be prompt for all appointments and rapidly furnish any information requested. Insist on having a polygraph test. You may wish to insist on a test given under the auspices of some agency other than law enforcement, depending on the reputation of the person or agency that routinely tests for the police. If your request for a polygraph test is not quickly granted, obtain your own test from a professional of impeccable credentials, one located by your attorney or recommended by an attorney who specializes in the practice of criminal law. True, the results of a polygraph test are not formally admissible in a court of law, but with each successive court appearance, your attorney can orally remind the judge that you "passed" a polygraph test that you demanded. Over time, this does affect a judge's thinking. As the case drags on and the accusation is unresolved, the impact on the judge becomes greater.

Finally, as time passes and the police or juvenile authorities do not resolve the issue, your attorney should continually ask the Family Court judge to hold a hearing on whether a molestation actually took place and to reestablish your access to your child if the judge finds that one did not occur. Family Court judges do not want to hold this hearing for several reasons. First, they know the Juvenile Court has controlling authority in this situation. If the judge should rule in your favor and the Juvenile Court ultimately renders a contrary ruling, the Family Court ruling is overturned and the judge is embarrassed. Second, judges are aware that the Juvenile Court, Juvenile Probation Department, and other county agencies have better investigative tools than does the Family Court. The Family Court staff is qualified to make evaluations based on a limited number of interviews, but is poorly trained and understaffed to investigate alleged crimes. Finally, family law judges are vulnerable to intimidation by law enforcement.

On more than one occasion a member of the District Attorney's Office or Juvenile Probation has called me with the following threat on the eve of a hearing: "If you hold a hearing while our investigation is in progress (at this point at least 40 days old) and make a placement of the child that I do not agree with, I will invoke my power under the Welfare and Institutions Code to remove the child from either parent and place the child in the public children's shelter, pending the filing of a petition to place the child in the status of a dependent of the Juvenile Court." That threat is quite intimidating because judges generally believe children do better in their own home, and no one wants to cause the suffering of a child who is uprooted from home and placed in a public shelter. It is interesting to note that on those occasions when I ignored the threat and held a full hearing (accompanied with specific findings of fact and an extensive statement of reasons), the threat has never been carried out.

If your attorney makes repeated demands for a custody hearing in Family Court on the molestation charge and enough time passes during which your child is denied access to you that the Family Court judge's sense of fair play and due process is offended, you may get a hearing. In some counties, the Family Court and Juvenile Court have entered into informal agreements or protocols that state that once the juvenile authorities commence an investigation, Family Court judges will defer hearing a matter for a given number of days to see if a petition is filed to make the child a dependent of the Juvenile Court. In Santa Clara County, the period is approximately 20 days, and your attorney's statement that the investigation has dragged on for 90 days will carry some weight. Unfortunately, other counties have unwritten understandings that Family Court judges will never act on a matter during an investigation by juvenile authorities or the police. The latter are given no time limit for finishing the investigation. In these counties, the plight of the parent falsely charged with molestation is indeed bleak, and months may pass while an accused parent is denied access to his or her child.

I suspect the problem of false or unsubstantiated charges of child abuse and molestation during dissolution proceedings will receive greater scrutiny by the legislature, and more public discussion. Currently, it represents too easy a way to put either parent at a disadvantage in a custody or visitation dispute. As an initial proposal, I suggest that the charge of abuse or molestation trigger an automatic appointment of counsel for a child. Although the child will ultimately have counsel if a petition is filed in Juvenile Court, that attorney (often the district attorney) may have a conflict of interest if involved in the prosecution of the accused parent. Moreover, that appointment may come, if at all, many months after the accused's right of access to the child was suspended.

DO'S AND DON'TS

Do...

- Ask your attorney whether custody mediation is confidential in your county or is "muscle mediation."

- Ask your attorney who will evaluate competing custody claims if mediation fails to produce an agreement.

- Concentrate on demonstrating to the evaluator that the children feel closer to you and would feel anxiety if you were absent for an extended period.

- Make an honest effort to determine with whom the children are more closely bonded. If the answer is your spouse, agree that he or she should have primary custody.

- Be aware that the evaluator may be watching the child's interaction with you and vice versa when you do not expect it.

- Ask your attorney of the judge's attitude toward equal time-sharing, if that is what you seek.

- Request that an attorney be appointed to represent your child if your spouse seeks to call him or her as a witness.

- Demand a polygraph test if your spouse wrongly accuses you of molesting your child and request the appointment of an attorney for the child.

Don't...

- Don't criticize the other parent during the evaluation for faults that do not directly affect your children; minimize all criticism — it diminishes you.

- Don't argue over whether time with a child should be called custody, visitation, or time-sharing. The child doesn't care.

- Don't ever refer to a child as "my" child in the presence of a mediator, evaluator, or judge; refer to "our" child or children.

- Don't allow your attorney to call your child as a witness in the proceedings.

- Don't assume your spouse can successfully program your child.

- Don't permit an evaluator to confer with the judge unless your attorney is present.

8

Child Support

How Child Support Is Determined in California

In California, child support is not set by statewide guideline, although it is often referred to as "guideline" support. Child support is determined by a mandatory statewide algebraic formula that is written into the California Family Code. Stated simply, when each parent's income and the time each spends with the children are entered into the judge's computer program, the computer applies the algebraic formula to the data entered and provides a support figure for each child. This figure is called the "presumed correct" figure of child support. Only in very few circumstances is a judge permitted to award an amount of child support that varies from the figure that is presumed correct. The judge must put on the court record each party's net, after-tax income, as well as the percent of time the judge determines that the children spend with each parent. Thus it can quickly be determined if the judge departed from the presumed-correct figure.

The computer program will further reduce either parent's net income for sums paid to support children of another marriage or relationship. However, unless the sum is court-ordered, the reduction in income allowed for those children cannot be greater than the presumed-correct figure for the children whose support is being determined. This is done in order to insure that all of the children of a paying parent are treated substantially equally. In addition, a parent's income — from which the presumed-correct figure is derived — may be reduced for a few enumerated hardships, such as extraordinary health expenses or the costs of raising children of another relationship who are actually residing with that parent. However, a hardship deduction for such costs is not automatic. The judge must find that the costs of raising these children are an extreme financial hardship on the parent, and under no circumstances can the hardship deduction exceed the amount of support awarded for the children whose support is being determined. In order to comply with this rule, the computer programs, if so set, will automatically put the legally required cap on hardship deductions for children.

(Once the judge determines what each party's income is and how time with the children is shared, grants or denies a claim of hardship if one is made, and puts this information into the computer, the result is quite automatic. Thus, under California law, most disputes will be over each parent's correct income or what percentage of time each parent really spends with the children, because once the judge determines those figures and puts them into the computer, the result is a foregone conclusion.)

It is also important to understand that the most competent family law attorneys have computers and one of two or three programs available to compute support. At a minimum, your attorney must have access to a computer and know how to use the support program properly. Many attorneys go over the programs with the client so that the client can appreciate how the program works and what factors are considered under the formula. You do not want to be represented by counsel who does not have access to these programs.

Expenses Don't Count

It is important to understand that child support in California is now based almost solely on the parents' incomes. The courts do not consider a parent's expenses. Every paying parent in California with average visitation (20 percent) who earns a net of $4,000 per month, where the custodial parent earns $1,000 per month net, will pay approximately $900 per month in support for that child. For two children, that parent will pay approximately $900 for the first child and $540 for the second child. All paying parents who do not see their children at all and earn $6,000 per month net while the other parent is unemployed will pay approximately $1,500 per month for one child and an additional $900 for a second child.

The omission of expenses from consideration in child support cases has been the law in California since 1984. By the early 1980s, Santa Clara and one or two other counties had income-oriented child support schedules that judges were encouraged to follow on the theory that they accurately reflected the reasonable costs of raising children at various standards of living. However, by 1984 the legislature concluded that most judges in California were not granting sufficient support to give children a decent lifestyle and free the custodial parent (read "Mom") from an impoverished existence. Judges were thought to be giving far too much attention to Dad's whining about debts and other obligations to a new family and too little attention to the needs of the children before the court.

(References to the noncustodial parent as "Dad" and the parent with primary custody as "Mom" simply reflect the fact that in the great majority of the cases that judges see, the parents stand in that relationship to the child and Dad is the higher earner.)

Legislators believed that too many children were being raised in poverty and that judges could do better by children of divorce. As mentioned earlier, women's groups took an interest in impoverished children and lobbied to improve their lot and that of mothers. They felt that when child support was inadequate, Mom wound up subsidizing Dad's puny efforts. Both she and the children were relegated to a life below the poverty line. Indeed, the concept of "feminization of poverty" was developed around support issues.

A Brief History of Child Support Law

Prior to 1985, judges in most counties examined the income of both parties, their standard of living during the marriage, the needs of the children, and the expenses of the noncustodial parent. The setting of child support had no standards or rules; it was mostly an act of intuition and guesswork. When the judge looked at Dad's expenses and said to Mom and her attorney, "There just isn't enough money to go around," that usually meant, "You and the kids are going to live in poverty, ma'am. Dad's bills and obligations are my priority." And the ruling, no matter how harsh, would not be disturbed on appeal. The setting of child support — like spousal support, attorney fees, and a host of other family law decisions — was considered a "discretionary act." This meant that the decision would not be reversed on appeal unless it was absolutely bizarre.

In 1984 the legislature adopted the Agnos Child Support Standards Act in an effort to increase and standardize child support. The act essentially removed expenses from consideration in child support cases. Each county was required to have a child support schedule that told the judges how much support to award after they determined each parent's income and the amount of time each spent with the children. These schedules were then thought to be generous in their award of child support. If the noncustodial parent's expenses did not permit support at the required level, that parent was expected to reduce expenses and work out a compromise with creditors. Thus, for the first time in California, an approach was instituted that put children first.

Judges tended to follow their county's schedule because if they did not, they were required to state their reasons on the record. If an incorrect reason for departing from the schedule was given, the judge could be reversed on appeal. However, substantial reductions in support were given to paying parents who spent substantial time with their children.

How the Law Works Now

Under the law in effect since July 1, 1992, each parent's income and the time each spends with the children are entered into the judge's computer, and the computer uses the statewide schedule to provide a support figure for each child. This figure is "presumed correct." The schedule is based on a mathematical formula contained in the statute itself. The statute warns judges that only in special circumstances should child support fall below the level required by the formula. If the judge inputs the parties' gross incomes into the computer, the program will calculate all taxes so as to provide a net income figure for each parent. The judge is required to put on the record the net income of each party as well as the percentage of the time the judge determines that each parent spends with the children. Thus it can be quickly determined whether the judge varied from scheduled support.

As noted earlier, the computer program will further reduce a parent's net income for sums paid to support children of another marriage or relationship if the judge enters that information into the computer. However, the reduction in income allowed for those children will not be greater than support permitted by the schedule. This is done in order to ensure that all of the children of a paying parent are treated somewhat equally.

In addition, a parent's income from which the proper support level is derived may be reduced for a very few enumerated hardships, such as catastrophic losses or the costs of raising children of another relationship who are actually residing with that parent. However, as with children for whom support is being paid to another parent, an upper limit is placed on the hardship deduction permitted for such children by a mathematical formula contained in the statute to ensure that all children of a paying parent will be treated roughly equally.

Why Judges Seldom Depart from the
"Presumed Correct" Support Figure

Picture the working reality of Family Courts all over the state. Under the crush of litigation created by the 1992 law and a lack of enough judges, a judge calls a morning or afternoon calendar of cases in which the judge is, among other things, asked to set or modify child support. There are 30 cases on a calendar that must be completed in three hours; some will settle and a hearing will not be required, but about a third will have to be heard. No other judge is available to assist in the event that time runs out before all the contested cases are heard. If the judge awards scheduled support by adopting the figure that is "presumed correct," the judge can hear about 10 minutes of testimony from each party, put a few figures into the computer, and give a decision. The judge can then move on to the next case. However, if the judge wishes to depart from the scheduled support, then:

1. The judge must find a "rebuttal factor" that would allow the judge to legally depart from scheduled support (the figure that is "presumed correct"). These are limited in number. They include the following situations:

   a) The paying parent's income is so high that scheduled support would exceed the children's needs.
   b) The custodial parent has the benefit of residing in the family residence that has a low mortgage payment compared with what a fair rent would be.
   c) A parent is not contributing to the children's needs commensurate with the time the parent spends with the child.
   d) Application of the schedule is unjust due to special circumstances.

2. The judge must state in writing or on the record the facts and circumstances underlying the rebuttal factor, the value of the factor, and the length of time the factor will be in effect.

3. Finally, the judge must find that the revised amount is in the best interests of the children and explain why.

Under the pressure of modern court calendars, it is unlikely that the judge will double the length of a hearing by getting bogged down in rebuttal factors. If the judge avoids these factors, basic data can be entered into the computer, and the computer will immediately respond not only with the scheduled support, but with a page containing every finding of fact necessary to sustain on appeal the use of the figure that is presumed correct. It is clear to me that the Legislature does not want judges departing very often from scheduled support and intentionally made it very difficult for judges in busy urban courts to do so. Judges seldom apply rebuttal factors on a busy calendar of temporary child support cases because recent case law requires so many factual findings that it is too time consuming. This is especially true of the "special circumstances" rebuttal factor. Moreover, rebuttal factors put the trial judge at risk for reversal, because if a factor is applied, the judge must explain how the result is in the best interests of the children.

However, a case decided in 1993[1] is worthy of mention at this point. The statute allows a judge to depart from the presumed-correct figure of support where application of the formula would be unjust or inappropriate due to special circumstances in the particular case. In a case named *County of Lake v. Antoni*, the trial judge made a child support award at only one-half of what he believed to be the presumed-correct figure. The judge justified the reduction by saying that the payor father had high bills and a stepchild that he voluntarily supported. The judge made no effort to comply with the statute by explaining how a lesser amount of support was in the child's best interest. On appeal, the ruling was upheld.

At the time, many of us felt that the decision, if widely followed, would threaten the very concept of child support determined by income alone without consideration of the parents' expenses. One major purpose of setting support by schedule is to remove the payor's bills as a factor in setting child support. If any case in which the payor has substantial bills is one in which the court need not use the presumed-correct figure of support, the whole concept of child support fixed by schedule is undermined. We feared that *Antoni*, if followed by other appellate courts or adopted by the California Supreme Court, would allow the "special circumstances" rebuttal factor to be a catchall by which judges could regularly ignore the presumed-correct figure.

However, no other appellate judicial district except that which decided *Antoni* and a later case with the same result[2] has permitted the payor's expenses or bills to justify a deviation from the presumed-correct figure. In case after case in other appellate districts since 1993, trial judges have been reversed for using the payor's expenses as a way to lower child support. Indeed, one decision said rather sarcastically that the legislative purpose in passing child support laws was not to maintain the standard of living of the payor. Trial judges have seen so many reversals for trying to use "special circumstances" as a method to avoid "scheduled" child support that they are quite wary of the special circumstances section and are unlikely to apply it. None of the cases which reversed the trial judge for considering the payor's expenses actually said that *Antoni* was wrongly decided, but said that *Antoni* results were not appropriate for

---

[1] *County of Lake v Antoni* (1993) 18 C.A.4th 1102
[2] *In re Marriage of Fini* (1994) 26 C.A.4th 1033

the case then being decided. Whether another appellate district will allow a consideration of the payor's expenses under different facts cannot be ruled out, but as of now, while possible, it seems very unlikely.

As of today the chances are over 90 percent that the judge will award scheduled support, and the chances are even higher for interim child support set pending trial. As a paying parent, you should make an effort to determine that sum and settle the matter for that figure unless your attorney believes that you have such a compelling case that the judge could not possibly award scheduled support. Not only is protracted litigation over child support apt to cost you more in attorney fees than you may save, you risk hurting your standing with the judge if you are seen as one who refused to settle at the figure the judge was so likely to order. Indeed, you may wind up paying the other parent's attorney fees as a form of sanction for failure to settle. This is equally good advice for the payee parents who do not want to be seen as grasping or using the children to obtain funds for themselves. A sanction against you for failure to settle what is often a preliminary issue decided early in the case will forever taint the file against you and can affect the judge's decision on other issues.

Can You and Your Spouse Agree on Child Support Other than the Scheduled Amount?

Yes. But before the judge can approve such an agreement, the agreeing parents are required by child support law in effect since 1984 to jump through several hoops. Whether the figure is higher or lower than that required by schedule, the parties must declare under oath either in court or in writing that:

1. They know their rights under California child support law.

2. Neither of them has been subjected to coercion or duress.

3. The support agreed upon is in the best interests of the minor children and will adequately meet their needs.

4. The children are not on welfare and no application for welfare is pending, or that the district attorney has approved the agreement by signing it.

If the parties agree to a sum below schedule, the paying parent should be warned that the other parent can, at any time, request the court to increase the support up to schedule without showing increased need or any other change in circumstances. (Normally, a permanent order of support cannot be modified unless the judge finds changed circumstances.)

Where the Real Battle Is Fought Under Current Law

Because the child support amount is almost a foregone conclusion once the judge enters into the computer the parents' incomes and the time each spends with the children, most child support disputes are over once the computer is activated. Judges will not normally spend time considering "rebuttal factors" that would modify the "presumed correct" figure the computer has spit out. Thus, most child support disputes will concern time-sharing and how much income a party actually earns or has the ability to earn. It is hard to exaggerate the importance of how time with a child is shared in determining the presumed-correct figure. If the obligated parent earns $6,000 gross per month and the recipient parent earns $4,000 gross per month, if the parents share equal time with three children, child support is $265 per month. If the obligated parent rarely sees the children so that his share of the time is 2 percent, then child support is $1,854 per month.

The struggle over time-sharing will follow two patterns. First, paying parents will try to make every effort to increase the time spent with the children so as to obtain a reduction in support. Indeed, financial considerations do and will promote battles over visitation and even primary custody. Paying parents trying to reduce their child support payments will quickly discover the joys of extended quality time with their children. Of course, the custodial parent, fearing a drop in support, will resist giving up any time with the children. Second, each parent will come to court with elaborate charts in an effort to convince the judge that he or she is spending more time with the children than might first appear. These graphs will count meals served, omit the time a child is at school or in child care, count overnights as full days, and other such manipulations that will benefit their position.

Such efforts are often a waste of money. As explained earlier, the 1992 law gives a smaller child support reduction for increased time with the child than any prior law that based the level of support on time-sharing with children. Yet struggles over the time spent with children are clearly on the rise. The desperation of paying parents may be so great that they will grasp at any means of reducing their monthly payment, whether the effort is cost-effective or not. A struggle over primary custody or visitation and the calculation of time-sharing can easily run up attorney fees of over $40,000. You should not let your attorney take you into a battle over any aspect of child support unless that attorney can demonstrate to you that you have a good chance to prevail and that the savings in child support over time will substantially exceed the fees that you will pay to your attorney and may be ordered to pay to the other parent's attorney. Otherwise, your attorney, and perhaps the other parent's attorney, will do well at your expense.

New-Mate Income

The importance of the change in the status of new-mate income as it relates to child support should not be underestimated. Prior to 1994, the law not only authorized judges to consider new-mate income, but encouraged them to do so when it would benefit children. Thus, if your child support obligation or entitlement was set prior to 1994, and one or both spouses were then remarried or cohabiting with new mates, it is likely that the existence of new-mate income affected the level of child support. If so, current law calls for a modification of the child support level.

The most dramatic impact of this change in the law occurs when the payor has remarried and the new spouse is a high earner. For example, assume Mom has an earning capacity of only $1,750 per month gross. Dad, who has custody of the three children, earns about $2,000 per month. He shares the children with the mother on a 70-30 ratio. Now assume that Mom has remarried to a man earning $95,000 per year. If his income is ignored, the three children will live on a cash contribution from Mom of approximately $343 per month. However, were the court permitted to treat one-half of the new mate's income as Mom's — which it truly is in a community property state — and vice versa, the children would receive approximately $2,000 per month from mom according to the statewide mandatory formula. The total allocation for the children from both parents would then be presumed to be approximately $2,500 per month, and the children would have a much improved lifestyle. Both the child-support figures and the assumptions concerning total support allocated from both parents for the children are provided to the judge by a computer program applying the statewide child-support formula, after the judge inputs the parties' earnings and the time each party spends with the children.

Not only may a judge not consider new-spouse income, but the judge cannot consider the standard of living of a parent and the new spouse if that standard of living is based upon the earnings of the new spouse. This came as a shock to your author who had relied upon a section of the Family Code, *Principles of Statewide Uniform Support Guideline,* which reads: "Children should share in the standard of living of both parents." A Court of Appeals, in a 1996 case, held that the prohibition against consideration of new-mate income overrides that principle of child support law.

The first thing that parents, both paying and receiving child support, should be aware of is that if child support was determined prior to 1994 by the use of new-spouse income, the figure set by the court at that time is now likely to be modifiable either upward or downward based on the change in the law. It is worth noting that the constitutionality of the statute prohibiting consideration of new-mate income has never been tested. In every other area of family law, we treat the earnings of either spouse as community property, and thus half of the income of each belongs to the other spouse. Only in the area of child support and spousal support do we treat the income of a spouse as community property but yet unavailable to pay the obligations of the supporting spouse, who presumably has a one-half ownership interest in the income. The unanswered question is whether this is an unjustifiable discrimination against children that denies them equal protection of the law under the United States and the California constitutions.

The impact of the prohibition on considering new-mate income in any given case can be huge. Assume, hypothetically, the following: There is one child and the father earns $110,000 per year and his new spouse is a homemaker. The mother, the custodial parent, has spent most of her life as a homemaker and has an earning capacity of no more than $1,500 per month. However, she has married a very successful entrepreneur who earns $300,000 per year. They lead an upper-class lifestyle that includes frequent vacations in Europe, dining in the finest restaurants several times per week, and clothing expenses of $1,250 per month for the mother alone. She and her new spouse are raising a child recently born to them and the mother has decided that she will be a homemaker rather than be employed. If child support is set solely on the income of the father and the unemployed mother, the father, assuming he has 20% visitation, will pay child support of approximately $1,600 per month including his share of uninsured health care expenses. That is a very healthy sum for one child from one parent. The mother's contribution to support is zero. Even if the judge imputes to the mother an earning capacity of $1,500 per month, child support is still a very high $1,400 per month. Only if the trial court could impute the mother's community share of her new spouse's income does child support become a reasonable $800 per month from the father, and each parent is then contributing about equally to the child's support.

Most judges as well as many legislators simply did not foresee this change in new-mate income law. Very few people realized that a significant portion of the public was seething with anger over the way the law was written prior to 1994. New mates looked upon their income as money that they had worked hard for and were offended by the notion that their earnings could be used to support someone else's child or used to reduce the support a biological parent paid for a child in the new mate's home.

Fathers' rights groups had long opposed the old law. They were not persuaded by the niceties of community property law. Some women's groups were not terribly enthusiastic about the old law, either. First, the general notion that one's net income should be the earner's to spend as he or she wishes had an appeal to women. In a country that is the most lightly taxed of any developed nation in the western world, Americans are cool to the concept of sharing income involuntarily. There was also the feeling among women that the old law made women less attractive to prospective new mates. Would a man want to enter a marital or cohabitation relationship if it meant that his earnings would be confiscated for the support of another man's child? Hardly, it was thought. Thus when Senator Charles Calderon (D-Montebello) introduced his bill that would prohibit consideration of new-mate income, a firestorm of support from the public arose and consumed any discussion about the needs of children in our society. There were very few legislators with the courage to vote against the bill.

The judge can consider new-spouse and even new-mate (nonmarital partner) income if it is necessary to avoid "extreme and severe hardship to the children." For example, the income of the paying parent may be so low that if the court used that parent's income alone in setting child support, the support would be so low that the children would be impoverished because the recipient parent also has little or no income. In that case, the judge is likely to be able to use new-mate income in determining child support.

A judge may also consider new-mate income where one parent refuses to be employed or employed to capacity and that fact leads to an extreme and severe hardship on the children for whom the court is setting support. But note, these exceptions in cases of extreme and severe hardship never apply if the recipient parent is the one who is refusing to work to capacity. In the example above, where the mother had decided not to work, no hardship at all was worked on the child because the father was required to pay more support. The child doesn't care where the dollars come from so long as they are available. However, if the paying parent refuses to work and recipient parent is of very modest means, then it is appropriate to consider the income of the paying parent's new mate in order to avoid hardship to the children.

Concealing Income

The dispute over how much a parent is earning or should earn will continue to be the most fertile field for dispute in child support and spousal support litigation. As in the past, the issue of earnings is often not whether one parent is lying about income but rather which parent is fudging the most. If both parties are salaried by large employers, room for maneuvering is rather limited. Each parent must bring income tax returns and recent, consecutive pay stubs to the hearing. Sure, Dad can be expected to swear that he'll never again be offered a single hour of overtime, but the judge is apt to compromise that claim and Dad will not succeed in lowering support beyond a reasonable level. The party who is seasonally employed or whose income is intermittent — the carpenter or the real estate agent — presents a more difficult problem. But the judge may go back three years in determining at what level income should reasonably be set. It is unlikely to be helpful for the real estate person to postpone all escrow closings until after the child support hearing. In fact, judges are never very receptive to a party's drop in income that coincides with the parties' separation. Although it may truly be related to emotional upset, it is more likely to be gamesmanship — especially if one party is asking for spousal support in addition to child support. Spousal support, not child support, is the real emotion-generator.

But if one is self-employed as the owner of a small business or a professional practice, let the games begin. And this is true whether the business is a corporation over which the employee has effective control or whether it is a proprietorship. The games start by asking customers to pay cash or by cashing third-party checks rather than depositing them in an account whose statement is subject to subpoena. Those self-employed in the building trades or providing care for children are skilled at receiving cash for their work. In one transaction, a parent can cheat both the IRS and one's spouse and children. If the business is a corporation, the parent's salary can be reduced while the company hides surplus cash in credits or receivables, or the parent receives loans from the corporation that are omitted from income computation and not discovered unless the opposing attorney asks the right questions. And, of course, bonuses can be delayed, and the parent then swears that the company is simply not in a position to pay bonuses this year. (This ploy is available to the employee of a large publicly held corporation, if management is sympathetic.)

Another popular ploy, which may take an expensive audit by a CPA to uncover, is to have the small corporation pay the parent's personal expenses and accordingly reduce his or her reported salary. The corporation pays all automobile expenses, country club dues, gifts to friends, home telephone bills, and certainly all dining out and health insurance. Some of these would not survive an IRS audit or scrutiny by the other parent's attorney or CPA. Experienced family law attorneys know exactly how and where to look for concealed income, and judges' healthy skepticism is helpful. Even if the exact source of undisclosed income cannot be discovered, the judge probably will not ignore proof that a parent's personal checking and savings accounts show a cash flow well in excess of claimed income. It should not go unnoticed by the reader, however, that the cost in fees for attorneys and experts to play these games probably exceeds any reduction in child support gained, even if projected for the remaining minority of the children.

Failing to Earn to Capacity

An equally expensive battle results when one parent fails or refuses to earn to that parent's capacity and the other party seeks to prove that fact. The judge can base support on a parent's earning capacity rather than on actual earnings, but only if evidence is presented that the parent has the capacity to earn more and is not doing so.[3] Even then the judge cannot use a parent's earning capacity unless the court finds that it is in the best interests of the children, according to a recent case in one appellate district. Battles over imputing a parent's earning capacity can take many different forms. Dad, an executive with a record of full employment at good and ever-increasing salaries, loses his job shortly before or after the parties separate. He has been unemployed for nine months, and Mom says he is dogging it. He says look at the hundreds of resumés he has sent out. Or at the time of separation, Dad loses his job and now works for another company at a lower salary. Mom says he is capable of earning more; or she refuses to seek employment, saying the children need her presence at home, relying on that portion of the law that effectively conditions her duty to work upon her duties to small children. Or Mom has a current or easily renewed teaching credential but wishes to go into real estate or be a salesperson at Macy's. Dad maintains the only way she can earn to capacity is to go to work as a teacher as soon as possible.

As a general rule, you cannot successfully obtain a ruling from a judge that the other parent is not working to capacity without the testimony of an expert in vocational evaluation and job placement who is capable of evaluating both the interests and skills of the parent claimed to be earning below capacity. To make a finding that one is not working to capacity, most judges believe there must be evidence of a given skill level and evidence that the skill is marketable in the community at a given income level.[4] Normally, only such an expert knows the demand in the area for given skills and what one with such skills can expect as a starting salary. A layperson does not have this

---

[3] *In re Marriage of Regnery* (1989) 214 C.A.3d 1367.
[4] These requirements are actually in the Family Code under *spousal support,* but there does not seem to be a good reason for an appellate court to say they are inapplicable to child support.

knowledge. Considering the expert's fees as well as the attorney fees spent in paying and preparing the expert for a deposition, I doubt that one can bring such an expert into a case for less than $3,000 to $5,000, so be sure the battle over earning capacity is cost-effective. If you are attempting to demonstrate that you are earning to capacity, be aware that experienced family law judges are not apt to be impressed with the mailing out of resumes. They have learned that it is frequent face-to-face interviews that lead to employment, not papering the area with resumes.

Children of Other Relationships

The problem of children of other relationships arises in a number of different contexts. Dad, from whom child support is being requested, may have remarried and fathered additional children. Or he may be obligated to support children of a prior marriage or relationship. Or he may have taken a new spouse with children whom he feels a moral obligation to support, although he is not legally required to support such step-children. Obviously, Mom can have support duties to children of a prior or subsequent relationship that will affect her ability to support the children of the parties before the court.

As mentioned earlier, current child support law recognizes that children for whom a party has a duty of support must be considered when child support is fixed. However, a stepparent owes no legal duty of support to a stepchild, and thus a party-parent's support is probably unaffected by stepchildren living in the home. At least consideration of stepchildren is not explicit anywhere in the statute. Perhaps a few judges will find it a "special circumstance" rebuttal factor by which scheduled support can be modified, but it is at least this judge's opinion that such an effort might well be error for which the judge could be reversed on appeal. Moreover, to consider stepchildren is contrary to the ethic that in the absence of an adoption, children should be supported by their natural parents.

It is worth stressing again that the amount by which a party's income will be reduced by support paid to other children, or by the cost of raising children of another relationship living with the party-parent, is often limited by the statute to a sum approximating the support that will be awarded to the children of the relationship then before the court. The judge's computer program will so limit the reduction, regardless of how much the party-parent actually pays in support for another child or the actual cost of raising a child living with the party-parent.

The struggle between old and new family for support dollars is an issue as old as the concept of child support. It has been the focal point of numerous legislative battles.

Suffice it to say that all judges will recognize that the duty to support other children must diminish the support available for children of the relationship before the court. The concept of treating all the children of a parent equally is now firmly established in the law of our state and the thinking of judges. Judges, however, are vigilant to spot deadbeat parents who claim a reduction in net income as a result of the duty to pay support of other children but are either in arrears on that duty or intend to shirk that duty. When the judge is suspicious that support ordered for other children will not be paid, the judge may fix an amount of support allowing the reduction requested but retain the power to review the case in a year or so and modify support retroactively if it turns out that support to other children was not paid.

Very High Earners

Child support law grants to judges the right to ignore the figure produced by the child support formula when the paying parent has such extraordinarily high income that scheduled support would exceed the reasonable needs of the children. It is unclear from the language of the statute whether this is an option or is mandatory when the paying parent meets the burden of proof of overcoming the guideline figure. Case law has made this "rebuttal factor" very complicated to apply. Before departing from guideline, the judge must first determine in writing or on the record what the presumed correct figure is under the statewide formula using the high earner's income. Then the judge must state at the exact level of the paying parent's income at which guideline support exceeds the children's reasonable needs. Case law is unclear on how one measures a child's reasonable needs other than that the needs must be consistent with the parents' standard of living. Finally, the judge must then explain how an amount of support that is less than guideline is in the best interests of the children. Many judges would rather opt out of the procedure.

What constitutes a high earner is not defined in the Family Code. It varies from county to county and even from judge to judge. In Santa Clara County (Silicon Valley), judges are apt to find someone to be a high earner at $60,000 to $75,000 per month or more. I suspect that the figure is far less in areas where incomes and the cost of living (housing) is lower, such as San Benito County or Placer County. However, in certain elite areas of Los Angeles housing costs are astronomical and it is common to see the children of those in the film industry or of sports stars cared for by expensive nannies, attending private schools, and transported, on occasion, in limousines. One judge who deals with cases arising in Beverly Hills says he is not sure that $1 million per year is a high earner.

Thus, before you offer to pay the reasonable costs of supporting a child at your standard of living, you must be certain that you are really a sufficiently high earner that the reasonable needs of the child will be less than what you would be ordered by pay if the guidelines were applied. For example, if your case were one that will be heard in an affluent district of Los Angeles, $4,500 per month is well below what judges in that area are accustomed to awarding the children of sports figures and film personalities who have lavish standards of living. So before you grandly declare that you can pay any amount that your child reasonably needs to meet your standard of living, you must be sure that scheduled support will exceed what the judge will consider the reasonable needs of your child. Again, your attorney must know what amount of child support the judges of the county are accustomed to awarding in high-earner cases, and your attorney needs to be familiar with the practices of the judge who will hear your case. $4,563 will sound like a lot of child support in Ukiah, but not for children at the Bel Air Country Club, or for the child of a sports star who lives in a $10 million home and owns two Ferraris. His child is entitled to his standard of living. Again the reader can see the importance of retaining a local attorney familiar with practices in the county and the practices and tendencies of individual judges in the county.

Child Care, Health Care, Private Schools, Travel Expenses

The issues of child care, health care, and private school expenses bear the potential to drastically increase the amount of child support a paying parent is required to pay to a custodial parent. Such sums are in addition to the basic child support set by schedule, which is called the figure "presumed correct," and may be ordered as part of an assignment to the custodial parent of the paying parent's wages.

Child care can be prohibitively expensive. Judges regularly see costs of up to $900 per month per child, especially if the child care also provides significant educational or recreational activities such as a summer camp. The judge can order child care paid in one of only two ways: shared equally or shared in a ratio of the parties net spendable incomes. The computer programs will use whichever method they are instructed to use by their settings. The ratio of the parties' incomes is determined by deducting child support and spousal support from the net disposable income of the high earner, and adding only spousal support to the net income of the low earner. In the most common case, wherein the low earner is receiving child support and spousal support, it probably makes no difference which method is used. By the time child and spousal support are deducted from the paying parent's net income and spousal support (not child support) is added to the low earner's net income, both parties are apt to have relatively equal incomes. However, in cases where the high earner has custody of the children, and the low earner pays child support but receives no spousal support, the attorney for the low earner should always ask that child care be apportioned on a ratio of the parties' net disposable income. In these cases the low earner's net income after child support is deducted may be less than half that of the high earner. Your author never ceases to be amazed at how often the attorney for that low earner either offers or agrees to pay one-half of child care when the amount based on comparative incomes would be less than 25 percent. The low earner is often harmed by this neglect on the part of the attorney. The contribution of the low earner may come out of income needed for the basic necessities of life, while the contribution of the high earner may come from discretionary income.

Health care is an issue of immense importance to children. The number of children without access to adequate health care is a national disgrace. Current child support law requires that either or both parents provide health insurance for the children if it is available at no or reasonable cost. Any employment-related group health insurance is considered to be reasonable in cost. If such health care is not available, or if a needed health care service is not fully covered, current law provides — as with the cost of child care — that costs will be shared equally unless the judge, on request, finds that allocation in proportion to income is more appropriate. Again, these costs are paid in addition to the basic support figure that is presumed correct.

Under California law, the judge may order a parent to pay for *private school education* or other special needs of the children as additional child support. Whether or not to make such an award is within the discretion of the judge.

Whether a party will be ordered to pay for the private education of children will normally hinge on what the parties can reasonably afford and what the children reasonably need. Californians, unlike Easterners, tend to be more public-school oriented, and many judges have the same orientation. In some school districts, available private education may be better than the public schools available. However, in California, private schools on the whole pay such pitifully low salaries to teachers that in some districts the public schools are equal to or better than the private schools available.

One socioeconomic explanation for the fact that public schools in California compete fairly well with private schools is that the better the private school the parties can afford, the greater the chance they will live in a neighborhood with high-quality public schools. The quality of public schools in an area is strictly a function of the income levels and the education of the parents (also related to income levels) who live in the school district. If you say to me Saratoga, Palo Alto, Newport Beach, LaJolla, or

Mission Viejo, I know, without looking at any figures, that well over 90 percent of the graduates will go to college and that they will score quite well on college entrance examinations. When you say Oakland, Compton, East San Jose, or Torrance, I know that the scores on college entrance exams will be lower and fewer students will go to college. It is a matter of income, which correlates closely with education. It has nothing to do with race.

However, it is often important to Roman Catholic litigants that their children receive a parochial education through high school or even college. Religious education is also very important to Orthodox Jews and fundamentalist Christians. It is highly unlikely that a judge will order the custodial parent to enroll a child in a private school, although on occasion such a demand is made by the noncustodial parent. Most judges realize there may be doubt concerning the court's authority to make such an order; and even if the order is proper, it will be carefully scrutinized by an appellate court. What a judge is more likely to do is order the noncustodial parent to provide funds so that the parent with custody may keep the child in the private school the child attended before the parties separated. In some cases, this may be in a child's best interest. The child is faced with a change in the parents' relationship, the probable loss of the family residence, and a likely reduction in lifestyle. It may well reduce the trauma to a child to be able to remain in the same school with familiar teachers and friends. In making the decision, judges will probably weigh the ability of the parties to afford private schooling; the special educational needs of the children, if any; the cost of the school; the reasons one parent wants to keep a child in private school (obviously, if both parties agree, there is no issue for the judge to decide); the length of time the child has been enrolled in private school; and the proximity of the school to the child's residence.

The judge will also have to try to determine whether the issue is important to the child's well-being, or whether the parties are involved in a power struggle. For litigants seeking to establish their power over the future relationship between the parties, the child's schooling provides an excellent opportunity to show that one can have one's way. In determining what is really going on, the judge, as in so many Family Court matters, will probably base the decision as much on intuition and feeling as on the evidence. A parent involved in the most blatant of power grabs will be able to find an expert who will come into court and support the child's need for whatever type of education that parent wants for the child. As you probably guessed, a struggle over education will be extremely expensive and can ultimately deprive the child of funds he or she might otherwise receive at a later date. Indeed, this is true of dissolution litigation generally.

Travel expenses may be ordered in addition to guideline support. These also may be apportioned equally or in the ratio of net incomes. However, the California Supreme Court in the *Burgess* case, decided in 1996, stated that in a move-away or relocation situation, the moving party can be ordered to pay all of the costs of travel for visitation.

Wage Assignments

Since July 1, 1990, the courts are mandated to issue wage assignments to be served on the employer of all persons who are under an order to pay child support. The judge no longer has the power to deny a wage assignment. The judge, however, may stay the service of the wage assignment on the employer. This may be done only if a year's history of timely payments without the existence of any arrearage is proven, or the obligated spouse provides by clear and convincing evidence that the assignment would be an extraordinary hardship. Such a hardship is very difficult to prove. Note that even if the judge has the discretion to grant a stay, it is not required. The ease or difficulty in obtaining a stay varies widely from judge to judge. Some feel that a wage assignment is appropriate in every case. Others want to give a paying parent every opportunity to pay voluntarily. If a stay is granted, it will be dissolved if the payee files with the court a declaration that the payor is in arrears in the payment of any portion of support. It is noteworthy that the rules of wage assignments apply to spousal as well as child support. Recently enacted federal legislation requires an employer in one state to honor a wage assignment from a court in another state.

In 1998, the California Legislature continued in its long tradition of thoughtless legislation when it passed Family Code Section 3653. It provides that when a party successfully moves the court to reduce child support on the grounds of unemployment, the order of the court shall be retroactive to the date when the motion was served on the other party or the date of unemployment, whichever is later. But, if, because the order reducing support is made retroactive, the paying party has overpaid support, *the party receiving the support is under no obligation to pay the money back*. Within a year the legislature saw the mischief of the statute and it was repealed.

DO'S AND DON'TS

Do...

• Consider making a claim for increased child support if the amount you receive was set prior to July 1, 1992.

• Seek sanctions if your spouse's effort to conceal income increases your attorney fees.

• Settle the issue of child support if possible. Court litigation will be costly if you are close to agreement. If you are not close, one side may pay sanctions to the other for refusing to settle near the support figure required by schedule.

• Consider attempting to modify child support if it was set prior to 1994 using new-mate income as a basis for the award or the agreement and such a modification would be to your benefit.

Don't...

• Don't hire an attorney who does not have access to a computer and child support program that calculates child support as the judge will do.

• Don't ever go into a court battle over any aspect of child support unless your attorney can demonstrate to you that you have a good chance to prevail and that the savings in child support will substantially exceed the fees that you will pay your attorney and may be ordered to pay for the other parent's attorney.

• Don't conceal income. The cost of litigating the matter will exceed any funds you can successfully conceal.

9

Spousal Support

There are several differences between child support and spousal support, not the least of which is the different level of emotion each engenders. Most parents acknowledge a moral duty to support their children. Indeed, most are somewhat proud of their ability to do so. But the average spouse does not acknowledge a moral obligation to support a former marital partner. To the spouses who are asked to pay, it may be called spousal support, but they know it as alimony. And they view alimony like American taxpayers view a welfare handout: The amount should be low and the term short. Parties seeking spousal support consider it a moral if not a constitutional right. You can anticipate that whatever efforts a paying spouse might use to reduce child support will be doubled in relation to spousal support.

How judges set spousal support distinguishes it from child support. As previously discussed, child support is normally set by schedule. After each party's income and time spent with the children have been determined, a schedule tells judges the appropriate amount of child support, subject to some fine tuning for tax considerations. Temporary spousal support — support to be paid pending trial — is often set by judges relying almost exclusively on a local schedule. This may be their only choice when confronted with the reality of coming to a decision in a 20- to 30-minute hearing. But it is error for which judges will be reversed if they rely on a schedule in fixing permanent spousal support at the time of trial. The Family Code contains a laundry list of factors judges are required to take into consideration, including the parties' income, earning capacities, expenses, and standard of living during the marriage — to name but a few. One major result of the prohibition on the use of schedules is that child support tends to be based on income only while spousal support takes both income and expenses into account.

Among the more important factors that the trial judge must examine in determining a level for permanent spousal support is the supporting party's ability to pay, the need of each party for financial assistance in order to live at the marital standard of living, the obligations and assets of each party, the ability of the supported party to be gainfully employed consistent with the interests of children in the custody of that party, and the extent to which the supported party contributed to the attainment of an education, training, or a license by the supporting party.

Prior to 1998, the cases admonished judges not to rely "exclusively" on a schedule in setting spousal support. Judges often determined permanent spousal support by first using the computer to see what spousal was by "schedule" and then making modifications to fit the facts of the individual case. This was especially helpful to judges new to Family Court and without experience in setting permanent spousal support. Indeed, some attorneys made the charge that while some judges wrote decisions that *said* that they had examined all the factors a judge is required to consider under the Family Code, the sum of support ordered was always the same figure as "scheduled" support. Then in 1998 the Court of Appeals decided the *Marriage of Schulze.* In that case the judge said that he had considered several of the factors in the Family Code, but the figure he arrived at was within $2 of scheduled support. The Court of Appeals politely said, "Judge, we don't believe you." The Appeals Court then went on to say that it was error to even *begin* with scheduled support as a starting point and then make modifications to fit the particular case. Indeed, the record must show that the trial court arrived at the figure of permanent spousal support by a "ground up" examination of the factors in the Family Code. The *Schulze* case is not gender-neutral. The *Schulze* court noted that permanent spousal support is normally lower than temporary support, and this has been your author's general experience. Permanent spousal support involves a consideration of what the high earner can afford to pay in light of debts and obligations, whereas guideline temporary spousal support looks only at income. To the extent that this assumption is correct, *Schulze* will be considered a victory for men's groups, because the supporting party is more often the man.

The only legitimate use of a computer program in determining the appropriate level of permanent spousal support is to ask the program to tell the user what amount of spousal support must be paid to give the supported party a net spendable income (after taxes) at the level the user believes is needed to allow that party to live at the marital standard, and whether that amount of support, if awarded, will leave the supporting party in an unacceptably impoverished state. If it does, then the judge will not be able to award sufficient support to allow the supported party to live at the marital standard of living. This will be the result in all but the cases of the most affluent litigants, because it is more expensive to live apart than together and there is seldom enough money to meet this extra expense.

Income of Supporting Party's New Mate Is Now Irrelevant

As is now the case with child support, California courts are forbidden to consider new-mate income when setting spousal support, if the new mate is that of the paying spouse. There are no exceptions to the rule. It was part of the 1993 legislation carried by Senator Charles Calderon (D-Montebello) and had even greater support than the limitation of the use of new-mate income in setting child support.

This law does not mean that an employed person who would be expected to be ordered to pay spousal support to a former spouse can voluntarily quit work and live off of the income a high-earning new mate as a way of avoiding the payment of spousal support. Although the court cannot consider the new mate's income, the court can still impute an earning capacity to someone who refuses to work. The court can then base support on that capacity. However, there must be testimony or documentary evidence in the record of what the unemployed party can reasonably earn with his or her present skills, or after additional education or training. The judge cannot say, "well, you must be able to earn the minimum wage." That is reversible error even if correct. Earning capacity evidence is often testimony provided by a vocational counselor acting as an evaluator. Vocational evaluators are one of the lesser expensive experts used by family law attorneys.

Since 1994, a number of payors of spousal support have been able to renegotiate the amount of spousal support that they are required to pay or obtain a modification to a lower figure from the court if the supported party will not negotiate a reasonable reduction. Those able to obtain a reduction in the amount of spousal support they paid were able to do so when, prior to 1994, spousal support had been fixed taking into consideration the income of a higher-earning spouse or new mate. If the spousal support you now pay was based on the income of your new mate, you may wish to discuss with your attorney whether a reduction might be obtained. However, you should be cautious, because other factors such as an increase in your income, an increase in the supported party's needs, or an involuntary decrease in the supported party's income could result in a higher level of spousal support even though your new mate's income is removed from the equation.

It is important to note that the new law does not change the effect of living with a new mate on the party receiving spousal support. Of course, remarriage terminates forever one's right to spousal support from a prior spouse. However, for many years now, California law has provided that if a party receiving spousal support cohabits with a person of the opposite gender, the supported person's need for spousal support is presumed to be reduced. The party receiving support has the burden at a hearing to show there is still a need for any spousal support. The concept here is that even if each of the cohabiting parties pays their own bills, two can live, per person, more cheaply than one. The new law on new-mate income leaves this rule unchanged. The income of the new mate of the party receiving support is always relevant. Indeed, spousal support may be reduced even if the new mate has no income and is a burden rather than a benefit. It is not unreasonable for the judge to reduce spousal support on the theory that if someone can support a freeloader, the need for support must be less than it was earlier.

Tax Consequences of Spousal Support

Since spousal support is tax-deductible to the paying spouse and taxable to the recipient spouse, judges must consider its tax consequences. Thus, payment of the sum fixed by schedule without regard to taxes will produce additional income or tax refunds from which the paying spouse can pay more spousal support. A portion of this additional income should be paid to the recipient spouse if that party is to have funds to pay taxes on the additional income from spousal support.

A consideration of tax consequences may also require a different level of spousal support because the paying or recipient spouse may be tax-sheltered by high mortgage payments or investments in depreciable property. The level of support fixed by the county schedule assumes a spouse's income tax equals the sum withheld from salary, or what would be withheld were the person not self-employed.

A paying spouse with numerous tax shelters may be entitled to a large refund or could claim more exemptions to reduce withholding. These additional dollars are available to pay spousal support. Likewise, a tax-sheltered recipient spouse will pay less on support received than would a recipient spouse without those shelters.

Computer programs are available that calculate the impact of taxes. They allow judges or attorneys to input the taxes paid the prior year by each spouse, or the average of several previous years, or the amount a CPA has testified will be the income tax due in the coming year. Indeed, the CPA will probably offer the judge a computer program that tells him or her what support should be set after scheduled support is modified based on tax considerations suggested by the CPA.

Your attorney should know a judge's reputation for departing from schedules in setting temporary support. It will also be very helpful to know how the judge approaches the task of setting permanent support. If you are the supported party, your attorney should offer computer programs to the judge who will set permanent support. Such programs are offered not for the purpose of determining the figure for scheduled support, but for the purpose of showing the judge (1) how much tax you will have to pay on the spousal support you receive, and (2) how much spousal support is required to give you the level of after-tax net spendable income the judge believes is appropriate.

This process is a constant reminder to the judge that you must have an award greater than what the judge believes you need to meet *expenses* because you must pay *income taxes* on the support you receive. It is also a reminder to the judge that the law requires not only that the judge consider the tax deduction spousal support will give the party paying you support, but must allow for the fact that you must pay income tax, both state and federal, on the support you receive.

Spousal Support: "How Long, O God, How Long?"

The duration of a spousal support award is influenced almost exclusively by the length of the marriage. Although I cannot explain why the length of the marriage should affect the *level* of the award, as the Family Code is written, the length of the marriage seems to be a factor applicable to both amount and duration.

Judges have essentially three alternatives in fixing the duration of a spousal support award. They can make the award payable *indefinitely,* leaving it to the parties to seek a modification or termination if circumstances change. (An indefinite award of spousal support cannot be modified unless a change of circumstances is established. Mere passage of time does not normally represent a sufficient change.) They can fix a support award to terminate after *a given number of months or years* — an act that has great appeal to the paying spouse. If the order is properly worded, the recipient spouse cannot successfully seek an extension of the time period. Or judges may fix *a conditional termination date;* that is, support will terminate on a given date unless prior to that time the recipient spouse successfully petitions a judge to extend the termination date. This conditional termination order is called a *Richmond* order, since it was first used in the case entitled *Marriage of Richmond.* A successful petitioning usually involves showing the second judge that certain assumptions made by the previous judge have not materialized, through no fault of the recipient spouse.

Once terminated, an order for spousal support cannot be reinstated. However, if the judge reduces support to zero but retains jurisdiction to raise it in the future, this is not considered a termination, but is what attorneys call a reservation of jurisdiction — a totally unwelcome concept to the paying spouse.

Statutes and case law found in published appellate decisions give judges some guideposts to the duration of spousal support. Since 1988, the Family Code has provided that a marriage of ten years or longer is presumed to be a marriage of "long duration" and that an award of support in such a marriage must be indefinite. An "indefinite" order is one that reads "until further order of the Court." The judge may also, in special circumstances, find that a marriage of less than ten years can be classified as one of long duration. There is very little case law interpreting this relatively new part of the code, but it seems clear that in a long marriage the judge can reduce support after a given period of time — indeed to zero if appropriate — but the court must indefinitely retain jurisdiction to increase support if appropriate. Whether the judge may, in a long marriage, set a conditional termination date as described above is now clear. At least one appellate district has held that a *Richmond* order is not a termination order and can be used in long marriages.

If the marriage is less than ten years and is found by the judge to be of short duration, prior and subsequent case law is helpful even though the statute is silent on the judge's alternatives in limiting support in a short marriage. (Since women typically receive spousal support more often than men, the law is considered a major triumph for women's rights groups.) The judge is free to terminate spousal support after a given period of time if it appears from the evidence that the recipient will be self-supporting by the termination date. In a marriage of less than six years, I believe judges can fix a termination date for spousal support simply because they don't believe a short marriage justifies longer support, so long as the period is reasonable given the length of the marriage.

Trial judges have been reversed in at least three cases for setting a termination date after an eight- or nine-year marriage when there was no reasonable expectation that on the termination date the supported party would be self-supporting. Currently, most trial judges will not take the risk of such an order. However, I do think judges are free to use a *Richmond* order in any marriage of less than 10 years.

It had long been thought that a judge would never be held in error for making an indefinite award of support in a short marriage. That myth was exploded in 1989 when a Court of Appeal reversed a judge for making a spousal support award indefinite when the marriage was two years in length.[1] In 1988, in another well-known case, the Court of Appeal upheld a judge who terminated spousal support after nearly five years of payments when the marriage was approximately six years in length. The wife had been brain-damaged during the marriage and would never be self-supporting.[2] This case seems to say that for a marriage of that length or less the court may fix a termination date for support although the recipient will never be self-supporting.

In summary, for short marriages the judge can fix support for a specific period, if reasonable, but as the marriage approaches the top of the short-marriage scale, the judge may be wise to use a conditional termination. And if the marriage is very short, it is an error to make an indefinite award.

A word of advice: If you are the potential recipient of spousal support in a marriage of longer than nine years but a month or so less than ten, you may want to at least consider delaying your separation until after ten years have elapsed from the date of the marriage. Such a delay could have a significant financial impact on your life.

A few words of warning are in order here. The Family Code provides that if a party receiving spousal support cohabits with an adult of the opposite sex, that party is presumed to have a decreased need for spousal support. Thus, if you want to avoid a motion to reduce your support but want to establish a relationship, it is best to maintain it in different residences. (The legislation is obviously a major triumph for men's rights groups.) And, it is established law that a judge cannot consider a cohabitation period prior to marriage in determining the length of spousal support. Thus, it is unlikely that a judge can turn a short marriage into a long marriage by adding a premarital cohabitation period.

Duty to Be Self-Supporting if Possible

In 1996, in what was considered by some to be a major victory for men's groups that lobby the Legislature on family law matters, the Legislature added to the factors that the trial judge must consider in setting spousal support the following new factor:

> The goal that the supported party shall be self-supporting within a reasonable period of time. Except in a marriage of long duration, (10 years +) . . . a reasonable period of time . . . shall be one-half the length of the marriage. However, nothing in this section is intended to limit the court's discretion to order support for a greater or lesser length of time . . . (Parenthesis added.)

---

[1] *In re Marriage of Hebring* (1989) 207 C.A.3d 1260.
[2] *In re Marriage of Wilson* (1988) 201 C.A.3d 913.

Huh? An additional statute once required the following language to be inserted into all orders of spousal support where the supported party is employable:

> When making an order for spousal support, the court shall advise the recipient of support that he or she should make reasonable efforts to assist in providing for his or her support needs . . .

The mandatory use of this section has been changed to use in the discretion of the judge. The first statute, as now written, adds little to existing case law. There has always been a duty to be self-supporting at the marital standard, if possible. The first statute does, however, give support to the concept of support being only for one-half of the length of the marriage in unions of less than 10 years. However, what little case law there is indicates that the one-half of the length of the marriage concept is not applicable to all marriages defined as short, and it flies in the face of the rule that a modification in support must be based upon a change in circumstances.

These statutes may, however, have the effect of creating in the trial courts an atmosphere that is generally friendlier to the termination of spousal support, if for no other reason than the statutes have restated what has always been the law and given statutory support of self-sufficiency as a "goal." This judge, however, without some approval in a published Court of Appeals decision, is not prepared to rely on the statute as authority for terminating spousal support after a long marriage and where there is no change in circumstances.

The one area where the new statutes may undermine current law is in the seven- to nine-year marriage. It may now be improper to make the award of spousal support indefinite if the supported spouse is employable. Such an order would appear to violate the newly enunciated goal of the State of California.

It should be noted that another recent addition to the law mandates the judge, when setting or modifying spousal support, to consider the criminal conviction of an abusive spouse and even mere "documented evidence" of domestic violence.

Suppose Your Spouse Voluntarily Quits Work and Is Without Income to Pay Child or Spousal Support?

The trial courts in dissolution proceedings have always had the ability to order spousal support based upon earning capacity. This is also called the "imputation of income." However, up until recently, it was thought that the judge could only do so if the supporting spouse quit work in order to avoid paying support. The court had to find such a "bad faith" motive in order to impute income. The concept was reaffirmed as late as 1992 in case where a former high-earning husband quit his job in order to enter a monastery. The Court of Appeals said that the trial court properly refused to impute income to him because he was found to be in good faith and was not attempting to avoid a duty of support. Support for the wife was terminated. However, that concept and result were rejected a year later by another district of the Court of Appeals in a case where a pharmacist left his employment to attend medical school. The Court of Appeals said that although he had been found to be making a good-faith effort to increase his income rather than avoiding his support obligations, it was proper to impute to him his income at the employment he left voluntarily. This idea was reaffirmed later by both another Court of Appeals case and by the California Supreme Court. It would seem that the current state of the law is that if a paying spouse voluntarily quits work or voluntarily reduces income, support can be awarded based on earning capacity and income imputed at that level. A bad-faith motive is not required. These cases have dealt with child support, but it would appear there is no logical and justifiable reason not to apply the same rule to spousal support.

However, the rule does not apply where one is laid off or terminated and has been unable to find employment for several months. Some vocational experts say that it takes, on average, one month of job hunting for each $10,000 of annual income an executive seeks to earn. Thus a judge may delay a considerable time in such a case before finding the unemployment to be willful.

It is important to note that it is not only the potential paying spouse who must earn to capacity. Recipient spouses must do likewise. However, if the recipient spouse fails to earn to capacity, the court can only impute earning capacity income if it finds the imputation to be consistent with the requirements of child care; an unlikely finding in cases of young children. So also the squandering of one's estate from which income could be generated can be the basis of a reduction or termination of spousal support.

Will I Have Time To Learn a Job Skill Before Being Required to Take a Job?

In one respect, the recipient spouse may be treated differently than the paying spouse. If the recipient spouse — usually the wife — has been a homemaker during a marriage of substantial length, the court may allow her time to obtain job skills before requiring her to enter the job market. If the judge is convinced that the recipient spouse is well motivated, it is not unusual for the judge to allow her up to three or four years to obtain a master's degree, attend law school, finish college, or complete some other equivalent training. If the judge insists that the unskilled homemaker take an immediate job as a salesperson in a department store or as a caretaker of children, the recipient may never be self-supporting and the paying spouse may well be paying support for life. However, with a teaching credential or other degree the recipient may soon become self-supporting, depending on the standard of living the recipient spouse enjoyed during the marriage.

Does Spousal Support Ever Increase?

The low or nonearner is entitled to support (so long as employed to capacity) that will allow a standard of living similar to that which the parties enjoyed during the marriage. The standard of living during the marriage is probably the most important factor in determining the level at which judges fix permanent spousal support at trial, or at which they recommend that support be set at the settlement conference.

Both child and spousal support can, so long as the court has jurisdiction, be modified after a change of circumstances, including a reduction in income for the recipient spouse or an increase in expenses for the child or spouse. In both child and spousal support, the party seeking a modification must prove a change in circumstances. If no change is established, the modification must be denied. The mere passage of time alone will not support a modification of either form of support, although the passage of time and the court taking judicial notice of increases in the Consumer Price Index may be enough to support a modification.

The major difference between child and spousal support is the effect of an increase in the paying party's income on the recipient's ability to modify a prior order made earlier at trial or settlement. An increase in the income of the noncustodial parent is always the basis for an increase in child support. Children are entitled to the same standard of living as their parents at any point in time until their right to child support terminates. This is not true with spousal support. If the award at the time of settlement or trial met the recipient's reasonable needs as established by the standard of living during the marriage, then a later increase in earnings by the paying spouse cannot alone be the basis for an increase in spousal support (the *Hoffmeister II*[3] rule enunciated in a 1987 case.) The recipient must, in addition to showing an increase in the payor's income, demonstrate some change in her or his circumstances. However, if at the previous settlement or trial the award was the best that could be obtained consistent with the law but was inadequate to meet the needs of the low or nonearner, then an increase in the paying party's earnings will support a modification without further proof of any type.

How does one now know whether an award made six or seven years ago met the recipient's reasonable needs at the time? Not foreseeing *Hoffmeister II*, judges' decisions did not discuss this point. Thus, in a current modification motion, hours can be spent on lay and expert testimony to determine whether an award made years ago was adequate to meet the recipient's reasonable needs at the time.

What does this mean to you as a litigant? If you are the recipient spouse, your attorney should demand at settlement conference or trial that the judgment contain a specific finding that the award is not adequate to meet all your reasonable needs. This finding allows you to return to court when your ex-spouse's career and earnings start to escalate. But beware if your spouse seeks the opposite finding: that the award does meet your reasonable needs. That means he or she intends to earn more — and not share it with you.

Spousal Support Versus Child Support

Some of the remarks made earlier on child support and attorney fees are equally relevant here. Judges have reputations for awarding generous or meager support. It is vital that your attorney know the reputation of any judge before whom the issues of either permanent or temporary spousal support may be heard. The reputation may be perceived as gender bias — an adequate support award for a woman, but not for a man. Years ago, one judge in Santa Clara County, on seeing the husband's request for support, said to the attorney (off the record) before the case commenced, "You don't really expect me to award support to your client, do you?"

If it is an issue, it helps to know how the judge is apt to account for a party's duty to support children of a prior or subsequent relationship as it affects spousal support. And your attorney will need to be even more vigilant for all the devices people use to conceal income — company loans, payments in cash rather than by check, company payment of personal expenses, to name but a few.

Finally, it is absolutely crucial that you always know how far apart you and your spouse are in settlement negotiations on the issue of support, and compare what you might gain at a hearing with what the hearing will cost you. The party that does not settle a case when the offers are only $150 per month apart is apt to spend far more in fees and costs than will be gained by continuing to litigate the issue.

---

[3] *In re Marriage of Hoffmeister* (1987) 191 C.A.3d 351.

Do's and Don'ts

Do...

- Insist that your attorney provide the judge with an accurate computer program on the consequences of tax shelters, including spousal support, if this benefits your case.

- Ask your attorney about the weight a particular judge gives to support schedules and tax considerations, his or her reputation for generous or meager awards, and his or her gender bias, if any, in making awards.

- Ask for a period of education or job training before you must find employment if you are a displaced homemaker.

- Settle when your offers on spousal support get close.

- Ask for a written agreement or finding by the judge that support agreed to or awarded does not fully meet your needs — if you are the recipient spouse.

Don't...

- Don't let your emotions control the litigation, or you will lose money.

- Don't separate after nine and one-half years of marriage if you expect to be the recipient spouse.

- Don't cohabit with someone of the opposite sex if you are receiving spousal support; have a more intermittent love relationship.

- Don't agree to a written agreement or judge's finding that the award doesn't meet your spouse's needs if you are the paying spouse.

10

The Family Home

Is the Home Community Property?

Community property law in California can be a very complicated matter, and it is not my intention to write a treatise on the subject. Suffice it to say that the chances are over 90 percent that a home held in joint tenancy is community property, although in certain circumstances if one party contributed the entire down payment or made payments from a separate property source, that party is entitled to reimbursement of the sums contributed, without interest.

Suppose the home is in the name of only one of the parties to a marriage. That situation is likely to create a serious problem for the party whose name is not on the deed. Often, when parties marry, one of them already owns a house where the couple will live. Over the years, however, while the parties allow the home to remain in one name only, the mortgage is being paid with community property funds. And during these years, its property value is escalating. If a dissolution action is filed, the spouse whose name is not on the deed is courting disaster. In dividing the value of the home, California law does indeed give credit for mortgage payments made with community property; but the spouse whose name is not on the deed will likely receive only a pittance of the substantial net equity in the home, and the spouse who brought the home into the marriage will realize the bulk of its current value. And this is true although the marriage may have lasted over ten years and most of the appreciation in the home occurred during the marriage.

If you are a spouse whose name is not on the deed and the mortgage is being paid from the earnings of one or both of you, you should insist that the home be placed in both names immediately, or that, with the help of an attorney, an equitable ownership of the home be arranged. Not to do so is unbelievably foolish. Yet the number of spouses who accept the promise, "Oh, this is half yours," or "We don't need to see a lawyer; don't you trust me?" — neither of which is worth much of anything in court — is legion. You have now been warned. If you let this foolishness go on another day, you have only yourself to blame. If you are involved in a dissolution your attorney will tell you so with eyes rolling in disbelief.

Must the Home Be Sold?

A sale of the family home is the usual disposition in a dissolution proceeding, and the proceeds are divided to equalize the division of all community property. Often, the home is the parties' only major asset, and neither party wants to grant the home to the other party and take a note in return. And they are aware that courts will not order such note giving and taking unless the parties agree to it. The sale of the home is sometimes by court order; but in the vast majority of cases is agreed to by the parties, who know that a judge will order a sale if they do not so agree.

During California's recession of the early 1990s, when defense industries laid off workers and executives all over the state, many families lost the substantial equity that they had accumulated in their homes. Family lawyers have told me that one consequence of the recession was to make settlement more difficult. Prior to that time, almost everyone had substantial equity in a home unless it was a very recent purchase. When the home was sold there were funds to equalize the division of property, pay the attorneys, and, unless the battle was protracted, for each party to purchase a smaller home. If a home is sold in a time of recession-deflated home values, it may be necessary to pay money into escrow in order to close a sale. The lack of funds from a sale of the home causes the parties to bicker more over all other financial matters and to be unwilling to leave a single dime on the table. Obviously, this attitude drives up the attorney fees and makes the parties' plight worse.

Of course, the particular circumstances may be such that a sale is inappropriate. There may be other major assets equaling the value of the home that can be awarded to the spouse who does not receive the family residence. Thus, the property can be equally divided without the sale of a valuable asset. For example, the parties may own rental property of such value that the home is but one additional piece of real property to be divided. Or even if there is only one piece of rental property, it may equal the value of the home. Or the business or professional practice when added to an Individual Retirement Account or a Keogh plan may equal the value of the residence, and one party may want the business or practice and be willing to relinquish the home in return. Indeed, more than one bitter attorney for a husband has been heard to say, "In Judge So-and-So's courtroom, the husband's practice and pension seem to always equal the value of the house." And, of course, pension rights over many years may have such substantial value that they will equal the value of the home when added to other property.

There are also those cases where one party has substantial separate property wealth and is sufficiently attached to the home to buy out the other party's interest. The purchase should be for fair market value, and a sum equal to a real estate fee should not be deducted from that price. If the court should order such a buyout, it would be at fair market value without that deduction. Such transactions, if handled properly, are called interspousal transfers and no tax liability arises for either party. However, the recipient of the home, depending upon the tax laws at the time the home is sold, may have some capital gain tax liability on the sale, and that will include gain accumulated when the home was jointly held. Likewise the recipient of an IRA or Keogh will be required to pay tax on gain or interest or dividends at the time the funds are withdrawn.

You must be certain that you and your attorney discuss all of the tax implications involved any agreement to divide community property so that you are not surprised at a later date when the IRS comes calling.

If the Home Must Be Sold, When?

Simply because the home must be sold does not necessarily mean it must be sold at the time of the dissolution. The party receiving custody of a child or children may ask that the sale of the home be deferred and the children be allowed to continue to reside therein as a part of their child support and to reduce the impact of the dissolution on them. This temporary family home award is often referred to by attorneys as the home having been *Duked* since the first case in which the concept of delaying the sale of the home for the benefit of children was fully discussed and approved was *In re Marriage of Duke*, a 1980 Court of Appeal decision.

Since the mother receives primary custody of children more often than the father (if for no other reason than that the father agrees to such an arrangement), the idea of a deferred sale of the family residence was a concept strongly endorsed by women's rights groups. The *Duke* case went so far as to make a deferred sale mandatory where the adverse economic and emotional impact on the minor children that would result from the sale of a long-established family home outweighed the economic detriment to the noncustodial parent caused by the deferral.

By 1987, however, another Court of Appeal decision[1] by a court of equal authority had put numerous restraints on the trial judge's ability to Duke the house. In an opinion clearly more concerned about the plight of a father who cannot reach his equity to purchase another home, this court said, among other things, that not only is such an award never mandatory, but the court appeared to say that expert psychiatric or psychological testimony is required before the evidence is sufficient to justify such an award.

By 1988, the various forces supporting and opposing "Duke" awards reached sufficient equilibrium in the Legislature to permit the passage of a statute authorizing California courts to defer the sale of the family home. But an award can only be made after a finding that such an award is economically feasible, and may be considered in lieu of a portion of child support. If the court finds an award economically feasible, then in determining whether or not to defer the sale of the family residence the court must consider, among other things, the financial ability of the noncustodial parent to obtain adequate housing, the tax consequences to that parent, and the economic detriment to that party.

Essentially, these factors must be weighed against the emotional impact on the children of the loss of the home and the ability of the custodial parent to continue in prior employment while residing there. Despite verbiage in the statute, it is clear that once a court finds economic feasibility, then the decision is discretionary. As noted elsewhere, discretionary decisions are not overturned on appeal unless they are so bizarre that the Court of Appeals can say that the trial judge "abused his or her discretion." A judge abuses discretion if the Court of Appeals finds the ruling to be one that no reasonable trial court would make given the same facts and law.

How are California judges responding to the statute? I have no statistics, but think some observations can be made based upon my general feel of things as a judge. First, it will be a waste of time for a parent with children in elementary grades or even in middle school to ask for a deferral until the youngest child finishes high school. Deferrals, if any, will be short and for a fixed number of years. It is advisable to look to the next change of schools as a target date, not graduation from high school.

A deferred sale will be unlikely in localities where rents are so high that the noncustodial parent must instead purchase a home and make a large down payment

[1] *In re Marriage of Stallworth* (1987) 192 C.A.3d 742.

that reduces the monthly payment. A deferral will be denied unless that parent can realize sufficient liquid assets from the dissolution to make a down payment on a home comparable in location, if not size, to the one whose sale is deferred. A deferred sale is also unlikely if the noncustodial parent cannot afford housing large enough to permit comfortably having the children in his or her care regularly. A deferral is also unlikely unless the children have resided in the residence for at least four years.

In any event, the issue of deferral is a judgment call by the court. Success on appeal is unlikely. Because of the emotion surrounding the family residence, you can spend a good portion of the equity in your home litigating this issue. If a qualified attorney (selected as I have advised in Chapter 2) tells you the judge is not likely to Duke the home, believe him or her and make your plans accordingly — even more so if you are so advised by a judge at the settlement conference, especially if the judge is the same one who will hear the trial. But if you wait until the settlement conference to settle this issue, you have already squandered thousands of dollars in hiring experts and taking their depositions. Your attorney should have a very good instinct, early on in the litigation, as to how the judges who might hear the issue are apt to decide it. Take your attorney's advice.

Who Gets the Home Pending Trial?

The question of who is to reside in the family residence pending trial usually triggers one of the initial skirmishes in dissolution litigation. If the situation is peaceful, each party has an equal right to continue to reside in the family home after a dissolution petition is filed. However, as you have probably guessed, the situation is seldom peaceful and unless one party walks out, each spouse will consider it a major symbol of victory to obtain exclusive occupancy of the home. Thus, the initial litigation may involve attorneys in a veritable race to the courthouse to see which spouse can persuade the judge to exclude the other.

California law permits either party to be excluded from the family home after a dissolution is filed, pending settlement or trial. But if you wish to exclude your spouse you must be able to show the judge that physical or emotional harm to you or the children is likely. Frankly, most judges know it seldom makes any sense to leave the parties together in an emotion-filled home during a dissolution. And there is usually ample evidence at the hearing on the issue for the judge to find that both parties are subject to emotional harm if they remain in the home together. So who gets to stay in the home? The party with temporary custody of the children, of course. Indeed, many judges will send the parties to Family Court Services for an emergency evaluation of who should have custody before determining who will have exclusive possession of the family residence. Only rarely will a party be able to persuade the judge to leave both parties in the house. Don't waste your money trying to succeed.

The preceding discussion assumed a hearing. What if one party wants to exclude the other party on an emergency basis without a hearing? In that event, the judge is asked to make an order based on declarations[2] under oath without hearing from live witnesses. Although most courts have a rule requiring at least several hours notice to the other side, such notice can be dispensed with if the judge is convinced that notice would probably produce violence against the party seeking the order. If so, one party, normally the husband, is ordered to leave the home immediately, taking only a few personal possessions (called a kick-out order). The judge makes the order without so much as reading a declaration from the party kicked out, but the order lasts only until a hearing can be held.

It is the husband who is most often excluded from the home without a hearing because to obtain an order without a hearing, threatened emotional harm is not sufficient. There must also be the probability of physical harm, and it tends to be drunken men who physically abuse women; seldom the reverse. The statute controlling such kick-out orders requires that there must be a physical assault or the threat of an assault.

Judges vary widely in their reluctance to order a person out of the home without a hearing. Evidence by declaration is notoriously unreliable. The most baseless or exaggerated accusations can be made behind the shield of the typewriter where cross-examination is not possible. So for many judges, the mere *threat* of violence is not sufficient. They want evidence of recent serious physical violence; it may be insufficient to allege that you were struck the year before. Every judge has had the experience of relying on a declaration that later turns out to be mostly fabrication. Judges also generally believe that, except in very unusual cases, the spouse in fear can find alternative housing for herself and the children, if necessary, pending the hearing. Indeed, an address unknown to the abusive spouse offers far more protection than a judge's written order. However, there is a strong general trend at work here. As more and more judges become better educated on the subject of domestic violence, their willingness to order the party engaged in violence or threatening violence out of the family residence increases.

You must also be aware that if one party remains in the family residence for a substantial period of time prior to trial, either party may be incurring a major

---

[2] In California, a declaration signed under penalty of perjury may be used instead of a notarized affidavit.

indebtedness to the other. For example, if the fair rental value of the home is far greater than the mortgage, taxes, and insurance on the home, the spouse living in the home and making those payments may be incurring a monthly indebtedness to the spouse who is not in the home for one half the difference between the fair rental value and the total of those expenses.

For example, if the parties have lived in the home for a substantial period and the mortgage, taxes and insurance are only $1,000 per month but the fair rental value of the home is $3,000 per month, then the spouse residing in the home may be incurring a monthly indebtedness of $1,000 per month to the spouse who has vacated the home (one-half the difference between $1000 and $3000). If 24 months elapse from the date of separation to the time of trial, the party in the family residence may have incurred a debt of $14,000. This is called a *Watts* claim after the case of the same name. While the trial judge has the discretion to deny such a claim or reduce it substantially for equitable reasons, your attorney has a duty to advise you early on of this possible liability so that you may seek alternative housing if you wish.

There is also the possibility that the spouse who is not living in the residence before trial is incurring an indebtedness to the spouse living in the residence. This is the reverse of the example given in the last paragraph. For example, suppose that the parties have refinanced the home several times and the mortgage taxes and insurance are $4,000 per month, but the fair rental value is only $2,000 per month. Under those facts the spouse not in the residence may be incurring an indebtedness to the spouse living in the property and making the payments at the rate of $1,000 per month. This is an *Epstein* credit after the case of the same name. What a rude awakening at the time of trial if the indebted spouse was not forewarned by his or her attorney!

If your dissolution began with a race to the courthouse for a kick-out order, you and your spouse may well be on your way to an expensive brawl neither of you can afford. Custody will probably be a contested issue, with the often-made charges of abuse. From there, you may litigate every item of property down to the children's furniture. But if you do, you should know that your chances of leaving the marriage with sufficient funds to purchase a home in as nice a neighborhood as the one where you now live are about nil. Your lawyer and the experts will have it all. Worse yet, your children will be permanently damaged emotionally.

Do's and Don'ts

Do...

• Get tax advice if you or your spouse want to buy out the other's interest in the home.

• Take your attorney's advice on the likelihood of a judge deferring the sale of the family residence rather than let emotion control you.

• Find temporary alternate housing, if you fear for your physical safety, until the issue of occupancy of the home pending trial is resolved.

Don't...

• Don't leave the home in the sole name of your spouse for another day.

• Don't try to obtain a deferred sale of the home until your youngest child has graduated from high school unless graduation is imminent or the circumstances are very unusual.

• Don't waste time and money trying to remain in the family home pending trial if your spouse has custody of the children. You will likely lose.

• Don't rely on last year's threat of violence to get you a kick-out order this year.

11

You Have a Duty to Treat Your Spouse Fairly

Under current California law, spouses stand in a fiduciary relationship to one another from the date of the marriage to the entry of judgment that disposes of all of the property of the parties. Neither spouse can take unfair advantage of the other; they are said to have the duties to one another that are imposed upon business partners. The most important duty is the duty of absolute and full disclosure.

Each spouse is now required to file proof that each has served on the other two declarations of disclosure, one early in the litigation and final declaration no later than 45 days prior to the first assigned trial date. The initial and final declarations must be updated almost immediately if circumstances change as to ownership and value of property. Along with the final declaration of disclosure, an updated declaration of income and expenses must be served. These declarations are, of course, signed under penalty of perjury. A judgment cannot be entered unless the final declarations have been served, or the parties have waived them in writing. The failure to disclose the existence of, or the *true value* of, a community asset in those disclosure declarations is grounds for later setting aside any judgment that was entered.

The major difference between current and prior law is that under the law prior to 1987, both parties were required to use reasonable efforts to conduct an independent investigation of the existence, classification, and value of each asset. If this was not done, a judgment could not later be set aside on the grounds of fraud. No such investigation is required under current law. Each spouse, in addition to disclosing all property and its value, must disclose all material facts and information of which the spouse has knowledge that would affect the value of any community asset. Thus, if you know of a potential zoning change that would increase or decrease the value of real property, it must be divulged. Indeed, if one spouse is aware of an appraisal on the property of which the other spouse is unaware, it may well be that the existence of the appraisal must be divulged. If you are aware that separate funds used to purchase property were commingled in a joint savings account, the law may now require this fact to be revealed. The danger in concealing this information is not simply that you must divide the property or the profits with your spouse when the facts are discovered — it is more than that. Under current law, if the judge finds intentional concealment of material facts, the judge must award the full value of the property or all of the profits, or both, to the spouse who was deceived. The law now imposes a 100 percent penalty for concealment that amounts to fraud.

It is conceivable that we may have reached a point where you should not enter into a marital settlement agreement that is not fair to your spouse. If, as the law now states, the parties will be judged by the standards imposed on fiduciaries and business partners, we may be at the point that any agreement that is unfair to one side is subject to being set aside by the court. The reason for this is that spouses don't normally consent to an unfair agreement. An unfair agreement results when one party has information that the other party does not have. It would appear that there is now an affirmative duty on each spouse to see that the other spouse is treated fairly. This is true even though the other spouse and that spouse's attorney have failed to investigate the facts. Nothing less is required of business partners and it is the duty business partners have to each other that is the standard for spouses up until all the property is divided and the issue of support is determined. Business partners are under no duty to investigate to determine the truth of what another partner says is true. One business partner is generally prohibited from obtaining any advantage whatsoever over other partners.

Do's and Don'ts

Do...

- Provide your spouse with a list of all assets and liabilities and information you have as to their value as soon after separation as reasonably possible.

Don't...

- Don't believe that you can take advantage of greater information about community assets and their value than your spouse possesses. It can cost you the entire asset, your half as well as your spouse's share.

- Don't fail to have your attorney file timely proof that the declarations of disclosure were served on your spouse. Your attorney may seek an agreement from your spouse's attorney to waive the final declarations of disclosure. That is perfectly permissible and may save you money.

12

Protecting Your Physical and Emotional Safety

Whether or not you remain in the family home, you may find it necessary to take legal steps to protect your physical and financial safety. During dissolution, negative emotions are running high, perhaps high enough to overwhelm the good judgment the spouses may have used in previous interactions. If your relationship has already come to physical abuse or threats of violence, if fear of a raid on the savings account by your spouse is disturbing you, or if you are deeply worried that the children might be removed from your residence, you may be able to obtain a court order that will be of some help. In these instances, an application for a temporary restraining order (TRO) is usually the starting point.

Keep in mind that such an order may be disobeyed. Defiance of a court order may lead to the jailing or fining of the disobedient spouse, but the order in itself will not guarantee your safety. You must also use common sense to protect your person, your children, and your possessions to complement the court order separating you from your spouse while tempers cool.

Temporary Restraining Orders

The subject of temporary restraining orders has been mentioned in earlier chapters (though not by name): the race to the courthouse to throw the other spouse out of the family residence; the race for a temporary custody order. TROs are orders issued by a judge without a formal hearing of which both sides are given reasonable notice. A TRO does not mean without the other side being present (*ex parte* in lawyerspeak). A TRO may or may not be issued without the knowledge or presence of the other side. Most if not all counties have rules for notice to the other side when one party seeks a TRO. The notice may be as short as three hours or as long as 24 hours. The "hearing" is then an informal meeting with the judge in chambers or a submission of declarations from both sides. But there are a number of exceptions to the notice requirement. For example, if the judge believes notice to the other side may provoke immediate violence, then notice may be dispensed with. Or the judge may not require notice if he is convinced notice will result in the conduct sought to be prevented. For example, the judge might believe if the spouse to be restrained had notice of a TRO ordering a bank to freeze an account, he or she would withdraw the funds before an informal meeting could be held.

Whether or not you receive notice of your spouse's attempt to seek a TRO may well depend on whether or not you have retained an attorney that early in the proceedings. Judges will far more easily dispense with notice to a *pro per* who the judge believes may not understand the significance of the notice (if indeed the *pro per* can be located on short notice) than dispense with notice to an attorney. The attorney's office can be reached by telephone or fax during business hours, and many attorneys are available after hours through answering services or message recorder-beepers. But more important, the legal community considers notice the very essence of fair treatment and due process. The judge knows that if he or she does not insist that one attorney call another with notice of an application for a TRO, or better yet fax the other attorney copies of the entire application, the judge may make an enemy or be the subject of talk in the local bar community. Moreover, if a TRO is issued without notice and then dissolved because the declarations on which it was issued are misstatements and exaggerations, the judge is greatly embarrassed knowing that the attorney who did not receive notice is aware that the courtesy of simple notice would have prevented the confusion.

Thus, if your spouse has retained counsel, it behooves you to retain counsel promptly. Your attorney should then determine the identity of your spouse's attorney and call that person with a notice of representation and a request for notice should a TRO be sought. Your attorney should also request, and confirm in writing, that if a TRO is sought your spouse's attorney inform the judge that you are represented and wish an opportunity to be heard. Your spouse's attorney will know that failure to so advise the judge would be a major transgression that could permanently hurt the attorney's reputation for integrity with both the bar and the judiciary.

If you do not know the identity of your spouse's attorney but suspect he or she will seek a TRO without notice to you, your attorney can notify the judge before whom the application will be brought that you wish to be heard on the matter. The judge's clerk should also be alerted. Good attorneys spend a great deal of time establishing good relations with judges' clerks and other staff members, knowing that occasions will arise where the clerk or other staff member can be very helpful if they want to be.

The need to retain counsel quickly to fend off a TRO runs counter to the advice I gave earlier about the need to do a thorough search before selecting an attorney to represent you. To avoid this conflict, I can only suggest that an attorney might be willing to protect you from immediate peril by agreeing to represent you in a TRO matter while you decide whom you wish to retain as your permanent lawyer. This temporary assistance by an attorney gives you a chance to judge that attorney's availability to you, ability to get a judge's immediate attention, and skill in dealing with opposing counsel. Don't judge the attorney on the basis of whether the TRO was granted or denied. The attorney doesn't create the facts and isn't the judge. The only fair question to ask is whether you received a fair hearing.

Two TROs are more difficult to obtain without notice to the other side. One, the kick-out order excluding a spouse from the family residence, was discussed in Chapter 10. Another order judges are very reluctant to enter is an *ex parte* order on the subject of child custody if they perceive that such an order will change the status quo and uproot the children. An unpardonable sin in the practice of family law is to prepare a declaration that either conceals or fails to reveal the fact that the order sought will cause a change in the children's living arrangement. Of course, if judges are convinced that a child is in imminent danger, most will sign a TRO changing custody. If such danger is not alleged in the declaration in support of the TRO to change custody, or if the judge doubts the reliability of charges made, then he or she is unlikely to issue a TRO that modifies custody without hearing from both sides. In fact, many judges will insist on an emergency evaluation by a qualified child-custody evaluator. The emergency evaluation may be no more than a two- or three-hour interview with the parents and children, but an oral report based on such an interview gives the judge far greater confidence in the decision.

You may note that I said a judge may doubt the reliability of a declaration in support of a TRO. In no other instance is an attorney's reputation and credibility with local family law judges more important than during TRO proceedings. Good attorneys know their good reputation with judges may be the most valuable thing they can give a client. If the attorney seeking the TRO has submitted declarations in other matters that were false or exaggerated, or has made representations to the judge that later turned out to be untrue, the chances that the judge will issue a TRO without notice to the other side are slim indeed. But if the judge believes from past experience that the attorney will investigate a client's accusations and refuse to present exaggerations or half-truths, the chances that the judge will issue the TRO without notice to the other side are increased tenfold.

Another word of warning: Do not fail to contest an application for a TRO simply because you don't oppose the remedy sought. For example, if your spouse seeks a kick-out order, you may decide not to contest the matter because you intend to move out anyway. Or you may conclude that you need not contest an application to change custody temporarily, because the change meets your immediate needs. But you may not know what allegations against you have been made in support of the TRO, and these allegations will become a permanent part of the file. If they are unchallenged and a TRO issues, a judge may assume at a later date that the allegations were true. At a minimum, your attorney might want to advise your spouse's attorney that you will agree to the TRO only if false accusations are stricken. Otherwise, the accusations may permanently taint the file against you.

Since July 1990, the Code has provided that certain restraining orders are automatic in every case and will be mutual. They are written verbatim in the summons and are effective when the summons is served on the other party. They continue until trial or earlier modification by the court. Both parties are prohibited from removing children from the state without written consent of the other party or a prior order of the court, disposing of property, making extraordinary expenditures without notice to the other party, and altering insurance coverage. The parties are free to agree to or ask the court to dissolve, modify, or expand these mutual temporary orders, or to issue others. But of utmost importance, the orders are not evidence of a history by one party of the conduct restrained, and no accusatory declarations become part of the file.

Emergency Protective Restraining Orders — EPROs

In 1997, the California Legislature took a major step in protecting the victims of domestic violence. It provided for emergency protective restraining orders that can be issued by a police officer right on the spot when the officer becomes aware of the violence. They are called EPROs (pronounced "eeeprose"). Such an order can be obtained against far more individuals than simply one's spouse. Among others who may be restrained are other family members, members of the same household, a cohabitant, a person with whom the victim has had a dating relationship, the person with whom the victim has had a child, and a person who is stalking another person, regardless of the relationship.

An EPRO generally works as follows: The order issues only at the behest of a law enforcement officer. An EPRO, like a temporary or permanent restraining order, can be obtained in a domestic violence action if the parties are unmarried, or the victim spouse does not wish to file a dissolution or separation action. The officer responds to a 911 call alleging domestic violence. The officer arrives at the scene, normally someone's home or a business, and speaks with the victim and any witnesses. Sometimes the perpetrator is present and sometimes that person has fled. The officer may make an arrest if the perpetrator is present. The officer can then pick up the telephone in any county in California, at any time of day or night, and within minutes reach a judge or commissioner. If the officer asserts that he or she has reasonable grounds to believe that a person is in immediate and present danger of domestic violence and relates the facts giving rise to the danger to the judge, the judge will then authorize the officer to sign an emergency protective restraining order which among other things, can order the restrained person not to contact, telephone, stalk, assault, or disturb the peace of the protected party, and to stay a given number of yards away from the protected person, that person's residence, and the protected person's place of employment. If the perpetrator and the victim are residing together, the EPRO can also contain an immediate "kick-out" order under which the restrained party must leave the residence immediately. In addition, the officer, if the judge so instructs, can award custody of the children of the parties to the protected party, and can deny any visitation by the restrained party. A violation of an EPRO can be punished as a contempt in Family Court or the district attorney may bring charges in criminal court.

An EPRO is valid, however, only until the fifth court day following the date of issuance, or seven calendar days thereafter. Before the expiration date, the protected party must personally, or through an attorney, seek a TRO (temporary restraining order) from the court that will remain in full force and effect until a hearing is held. California Family Courts now have a "help center" to assist those without an attorney in turning the EPRO into a TRO The hearing must be scheduled within 25 days.

This section on EPROs cannot possibly cover all of law on the subject, but is merely intended to advise the reader that emergency help, which includes restraining orders, is available at any time. Some departments of law enforcement seek EPROs as a matter of course in any situation where the officer believes that domestic violence occurs. The four judges and two commissioners of my Family Court probably each authorize at least one EPRO per day during business hours. After business hours, a duty judge may be inundated with so many telephone requests that it is almost impossible to get a good night's sleep. For reasons that are not entirely clear, other departments of law enforcement seem to seldom make requests for EPROs. Those officers that use them believe the process works in almost all cases to protect potential victims of domestic violence. It is up to the courts, the counties, the cities, and the departments of law enforcement to see that officers are fully educated in the value of using EPROs.

Contempt Actions

A contempt of court action is the method by which temporary and permanent court orders are enforced. However, the judicial system is able to function only because most citizens feel morally bound to obey court orders. This is true of our laws in general — most Americans feel it is wrong to violate them. When our laws do not reflect the common moral views of the society, trouble develops for the legal system. (Prohibition is a good example.) If fear of punishment is the only reason citizens obey a law, then wholesale violations can be expected (e.g., the 55-mile-per-hour speed limit).

If you are found in contempt of court because of a violation of a court order, it is a serious matter. Not only are you vulnerable to a jail sentence and fine, but your file is permanently tainted and your integrity and credibility damaged on all issues. Because violations of court orders are considered matters of great seriousness by judges and attorneys alike, a file is also permanently tainted against a party who brings a frivolous contempt action, or who is perceived as using the contempt weapon as the first rather than the last resort in dispute resolution.

A contempt charge should only be brought for the most serious conduct, which cannot be prevented in any other way; and your ability to prove the contempt must be absolutely certain. If the judge believes a contempt charge was brought only to gain an advantage in the litigation, not only may your credibility be permanently harmed, but you may be ordered to pay all your spouse's attorney fees incurred in defending the charge. Unless unusual circumstances exist, the loser in a contempt action pays the other party's attorney fees.

Most contempt actions are brought for failure to pay support and failure to obey custody and visitation orders.[1] Visitation is one area where the party bringing the charge can get into trouble. Before you bring a contempt action for even a continuing

---

[1] One cannot be held in contempt of court for the failure to pay a simple debt to one's spouse or former spouse. This country does not have debtors' prisons.

pattern of returning a child an hour or so late, you should be certain the evidence will reveal you have made all reasonable efforts to end the conduct without court action, and there are no reasonable explanations for the conduct. Physical violence is seldom the subject of a contempt action because orders against assaultive behavior are not often violated, and if they are, the district attorney will normally file criminal charges.

If you are charged with being in contempt of court, take the matter seriously. Unless you are sentenced to six months or more, you do not have the right to a jury trial. When jail is used to punish contempt, seldom is the sentence for more than a few days. In Family Court, people cited for contempt are not criminals, but are, by and large, law-abiding citizens. A few hours in jail is a truly horrendous experience. If the judge cannot modify that person's behavior with a sentence of four or five days, the judge will never be able to modify it.

Four simple facts must be established beyond a reasonable doubt before a person can be held in contempt.

1. A directive order must have been established — for example, to pay child support in a given amount per month or to grant visitation at certain times. Beware such orders as "the proceeds from the sale of the home will be equally divided between the parties" — it may not be sufficiently directive since it doesn't say who is to divide the proceeds. An escrow officer? A party? Does "divide" also mean "to distribute"? If an order is poorly drafted, the blame normally lies with the attorney preparing the order for the judge's signature. But the existence of a directive order is normally established simply by asking the judge to take notice of a prior order in the file that is in front of the judge. It takes 15 seconds at most.

2. The party charged with violating the order must have had knowledge of the order violated. This can be proven by asking the judge to note that the order reveals both parties were present in court when the order was made verbally, or by testimony that the party cited for contempt admitted receiving a copy of the order, or took action consistent with knowledge of the order, such as paying support for the first three months after the order. This should take less than two minutes to verify.

3. The order must have been violated. In cases involving failure to pay support, this requires no more than testimony that the sum ordered was not received. In cases involving violations of visitation orders, the fact of the violation is the

major issue in what is likely to be a swearing match between the parties. ("You were late." "I was not.") Since the violation must be established beyond a reasonable doubt, the party bringing the charge should have a witness to the violation.

4. Contempt orders for child and spousal support differ radically from other orders for which a contempt holding is sought. The charging party need not establish ability to comply as part of that party's case. The charging party need only provide a directive order, knowledge of the order, and a failure to pay. It is up to the party charged to prove by a preponderance of the evidence that he or she did not have the ability to pay.

However, the charging party must be prepared with proof of ability to pay in the event that the party charged does offer evidence of inability to pay. In child and spousal support cases, proof of ability to pay may be quite simple. The employer's pay records can be subpoenaed into court, or the charging party may be able to testify of personally observing the other party at work, and of knowledge of what the job paid during the marriage. If the party charged with contempt is self-employed, or moves from job to job, ability to pay is very hard to prove. How does one know where the party charged is employed, if at all? Private investigators are prohibitively expensive for a support-collection matter. How does one establish that the business provided income sufficient to meet bare necessities as well as pay support? In a spousal support case, a judge can order support based upon ability to earn, but the judge may not base contempt on such ability. A finding of contempt in spousal support cases requires a finding that the party cited for contempt (the citee) had funds in his or her control that could have been used to comply with the order. As this book goes to the publisher, one cannot be held in contempt of court in a spousal support matter for failure to seek and find employment.

However, child support is now an entirely different matter. In a major case that changed what most judges believed the law to be, the California Supreme Court in 1998 held that a person can be held in contempt of court if that person fails to pay child support and also fails to heed the order of the judge to seek and find employment. Not only can the judge order child support based on earning capacity, but now the judge can base contempt on that earning capacity. It is likely that as a result of this ruling, judges, and especially commissioners hearing cases to enforce child support orders brought by the district attorney, may, as a matter of routine practice, order any unemployed person who is behind in child support payments and is cited for contempt to seek, find, and hold employment and to return to court on a given date to report on his or her efforts to find employment and to stand trial for contempt if the person is not employed. At that hearing, if support is still in arrears, the burden will be on that party (the citee) to prove all reasonable efforts to find employment. If the judge does not believe that the citee has established that he or she has made all reasonable efforts to find and hold employment, then the citee can be held in contempt.

Courts will likely have standard written "employment efforts" orders that will be served on the unemployed citees at the time they first appear in court. This will not delay the proceedings because contempts seldom are heard at the citee's first appearance. At that appearance, citees must be advised of their rights, including the right to an attorney at public expense if they cannot afford an attorney. Since most of the unemployed cannot afford to pay an attorney, they must be sent to an attorney designated by the judge or the public defender, who will need time to prepare to defend the charges.

Despite the rather straightforward proof necessary to establish contempt, a substantial portion of the Family Law Bar comes to court poorly prepared to establish all three factors and offer rebuttal evidence on the fourth. The worst practitioners gloss over the possible need to prove ability to comply with a support order, or try to call the citee as a witness against himself or herself in order to establish proof of ability to pay, in violation of the accused's constitutional right against self-incrimination. But even competent practitioners do not carefully think through their proof and try to rely on inadmissible hearsay — "My friend Sue told me she saw John at work." You are perfectly justified in asking your attorney how much experience he or she has had in proving contempts. The consequences of losing, as explained earlier, can bias the entire litigation against you.

I also believe family law attorneys are often not as skilled as criminal attorneys in the defense of contempt charges. Please note that this is the *only* area of family law where extensive criminal law experience is likely to be helpful. Criminal lawyers often approach other family law issues with such an adversarial stance that everyone in the system — judge, opposing attorney, court staff — is horrified by their conduct, and thus the client is poorly served. But criminal lawyers, skilled in the use of the Evidence Code and keenly aware of the constitutional requirements for conviction in criminal matters, seldom miss an opportunity to help their client in a contempt hearing. For example, they know that bank records are hearsay unless someone from the bank appears in court during the hearing and identifies them as bank business records. They also know that in either a civil or criminal contempt hearing, the judge will strictly enforce the rules of evidence.

Criminal attorneys know how to test the sufficiency of the other party's case by making a motion to discharge the contempt after all evidence against the client has been presented, but before the client must decide whether or not to testify. The motion must be granted unless all three elements discussed above have been established. Attorneys trained in criminal law know the perils of having the charged party testify without first making such a motion. The client unwittingly may fill in gaps in the case. For example, there may be no evidence that the citee had knowledge of the order. But if the citee testifies, the citee may be forced to admit receiving a copy of the order in the mail. However, if the motion to discharge the contempt is brought before the citee testifies, then if knowledge of the order has not been proven, the charge of contempt will be dismissed by the judge before the client risks testifying in his or her own defense.

In any event, if you are charged with being in contempt of court, candidly discuss with your attorney his or her experience in the defense of contempt actions, and inquire whether it is in your best interest for an experienced criminal attorney to handle this one aspect of the case.

Do's and Don'ts

Do...

- Retain counsel quickly, if only temporarily, if you fear your spouse will attempt to get a TRO without notice to you.

- Make every effort to learn the identity of your spouse's attorney if you believe your spouse will seek a TRO.

- Seek representation by a qualified criminal lawyer if your family law attorney lacks experience in defending contempt actions.

Don't...

- Don't attempt to get a TRO that modifies the custody status without making it clear to the judge that the order sought would effect a custody change.

- Don't exaggerate in your declaration in support of a TRO.

- Don't fail to contest a TRO or injunction application sought by your spouse simply because you don't oppose the request.

- Don't bring a contempt charge unless you can establish the four facts beyond a reasonable doubt and demonstrate that you have exhausted all other possible efforts to gain compliance.

13

Attorney Fees

No issue in family law outranks attorney fees as regards the importance of your attorney knowing the inclinations, habits, and preferences of the judge who will hear the matter. The California Family Law Act provides that the court may order one party to pay all or part of the attorney fees and costs of the other party. Such an award, or the refusal to make such an award, is what is known as "in the discretion of the court." This means that the decision of the trial judge on this issue will not be overturned on appeal unless it is so outrageous that the reviewing court can say that no reasonable judge would make a like award. Your attorney will tell you that a reversal is highly unlikely. Trial judges are virtually never reversed on appeal on the ground that an award was either too great or too meager.

Judges who spend any significant time hearing family law matters develop reputations not only as to whether they will award a substantial sum of money as attorney fees in appropriate cases, but also for the presence or absence of gender bias on this issue; that is, reputations for whether husbands are as readily awarded attorney fees from higher-earning wives as wives are awarded fees from higher-earning husbands. Family law attorneys will tell you that, generally, judges who have never been in private practice, but have only worked for government at some level, award very meager attorney fees.

Any competent local family law specialist (or active practitioner) knows the reputation of any given judge regarding attorney fees. Indeed, reputations become so detailed that attorneys sometimes claim to know a mathematical formula that certain judges apply to every case in which the attorney fees are in dispute. Judges' reputations on this issue are as available in the Family Law Bar as on the issue of spousal support.

The Basis of Fee Awards

Under the Family Law Act as now embodied in the Family Code, an award of fees is to be based on the value of the legal services rendered, as well as the ability of one party to assist the other and the need of the other party to have such assistance. It is obvious that a judge's willingness to award substantial attorney fees in an appropriate case is a matter of great concern to women generally and women's rights groups in particular. In the traditional marriage, it is usually the wife who will be seeking attorney fees from the husband. She may be a homemaker; but even if she is employed, she is unlikely to have earnings or earning capacity equal to her husband's. Women in traditional marriages often have not sought or attained the educational level of their husbands; and even if they have, women often earn less than men for work of comparable value.

Although it is more often the wife who seeks an award of attorney fees (as with spousal support), the statute granting the court authority to award attorney fees is gender-neutral. If the husband is the low earner or is a homemaker and in need of help with his attorney fees, he is as legally entitled to help as a wife in the same circumstances.

Attorney Fees: An Emotional Issue

If you are the spouse from whom attorney fees are demanded, you need to be sure what your attorney is offering in settlement negotiations. The issue of attorney fees is often the most emotional issue in a dissolution action. The higher-earning spouse will likely consider such fees the bitterest pill he or she must swallow during the entire litigation. This feeling is a virtual certainty when the high earner does not want the marriage dissolved but the low earner has found a new companion and wants a dissolution. In this situation, the high earner will view the spouse's attorney as a person who is unnecessarily wrecking the marriage and whom the high earner must now compensate at the rate of $250 to $600 per hour so the attorney can complete the destruction. Indeed, the issue is often emotional enough to prevent the settlement of a case where the parties have agreed or can agree on all other issues, including spousal support.

Fees Often Are Disguised

Family law attorneys, aware of the strong emotions aroused by this issue, often structure settlements so that attorney fees are omitted from the agreement. It is common to hear an offer such as the following from the high earner's attorney to the other attorney during settlement negotiations: "I know if we go to trial the court will order my client to pay some amount of your client's attorney fees, but he'll never voluntarily agree to make such a payment as part of a settlement. Why don't we give your client X dollars greater liquid community property assets? Your client can use the money to pay you, but the agreement will not expressly provide for attorney fees."

There is nothing wrong with such a proposal so long as both parties are aware that there is a direct trade-off of community property for attorney fees. In addition, the high earner should be informed of, and consent to, such an offer before it is made. Having heard hundreds of such proposals during my career, I must say that I have doubts whether most of the high earners (namely, husbands) have given prior consent to such an offer, if indeed they were ever informed of the true nature of the settlement. Thus, a word of warning to the party from whom an award of attorney fees is demanded: Be sure that you are not unknowingly paying attorney fees in the guise of spousal support or community property.

It is just as common for one attorney to say to the other: "Why don't we settle all issues other than attorney fees and then submit that one issue to the judge in a 15-minute trial? My client will pay fees to your client if he is ordered to do so, but if I ask him to pay voluntarily he will not only refuse but will probably back away from the settlement of other issues."

Again, there is nothing wrong with such an agreement so long as the client from whom fees are requested is aware that his or her attorney believes the judge is, in fact, going to award fees to the other side. If the client is not so informed, it is highly improper. If properly informed, the client could ask the attorney to predict what the judge will award and then authorize settlement at a figure that is slightly lower or at the low end of the predicted range. It is improper for the attorney not to give the client that option on the assumption that it will be refused.

If your attorney wants to submit the single issue of fees to the judge for decision, you should inquire whether your attorney thinks such an action is in your best interest or is a *pro forma* act that will result in your being ordered to pay a figure the judge has already suggested during settlement negotiations.

Fees Seldom Are Equalized

The reality of Family Court is that in very few cases does the attorney for the low earner receive fees equal to those received by the high earner's attorney. The reason for this is unclear. The theoretical basis for the statute enabling courts to award attorney fees is quite solid. If low earners (as compared to their spouses) or nonearning homemakers are to have legal representation as capable and competent as their spouses, their attorneys must be able to rely on an award of fees by the court from higher-earning spouses of sufficient magnitude that their fees are comparable to those paid to attorneys for the high earners. If they are unable to rely on such an award, attorneys will decline to represent low earners in a marriage relationship; and since the low earner is usually the wife, married women generally will have less capable attorneys than their spouses. These attorneys will then refuse to take the cases of low-earning married women unless the client can pay them a $5,000 to $20,000 retainer, which the client may or may not be able to do.

A Potential Conflict of Interest

When the wife becomes legally obligated during litigation to pay fees she cannot afford, a major conflict of interest between the wife and her attorney may arise. (This is also true of husbands, but less often.) For example, the wife may want to remain in the family residence for a year or so after the dissolution for the benefit of children who would be disrupted by a change in schools. Yet the proceeds from a sale of the family residence may be the only way liquid assets can be generated from which her attorney (whose fees may now exceed $30,000) can be paid. Attorneys who want t be timely paid their fees may not be sympathetic to the needs of the children to remain in the home. They do not relish the concept of having their bill paid at $200 a month from a client who can barely eek this sum out of her spousal support and meager earnings, if any. Thus, if you want to remain in the family residence for some period after the dissolution or to buy out your spouse's interest in the home, you need to have an early and frank discussion with your attorney about the conflict that may arise if he or she must look to the home for payment of fees. And you should never assume, because you have X dollars in liquid assets, your attorney's charges will not exceed that sum. Attorney fees are notoriously unpredictable in matrimonial litigation and are almost always higher than anticipated — sometimes double or triple.

Several factors may account for the low earner's attorney being undercompensated or failing to receive an award commensurate with the fee paid to the other party's attorney. The first is that the low earner is always perceived as having *some* ability to pay attorney fees, and thus the high earner is ordered to pay only a portion of the low earner's fees — between 25 and 60 percent is common. This is true even if the wife is a homemaker and has no income. Most county schedules used in California recommend temporary spousal support of 40 percent of the net income of the high earner, less 50 percent of the net income of the low earner. When the judge sees that up to 40 percent of the high earner's net income goes to spousal support, the incomes look somewhat comparable. The appearance of equality may be deceptive, however. Of course, the judge may not follow the 40 percent schedule. But even if the judge does, the temporary spousal support award is normally not enough to allow the recipient to maintain the marital standard of living; and it is seldom set to furnish funds for the payment of fees.

If the parties have led a lifestyle that, despite upper-middle-class earnings, has left them with no liquid savings, the situation is more difficult for the low earner's attorney because the judge cannot identify a fund from which fees can be paid and is loathe to put the low earner's attorney in competition with the low earner and perhaps the children for the dollars of the high earner. The judge, seeing relative equivalency of income and no identifiable source of funds for the payment of fees, is apt to be either very conservative in the award, or, as we shall discuss later, to put off an award of fees hoping the sale of property will generate funds from which fees can be paid. In any event, if you are the low earner and your attorney tells you there is no possibility you will receive an order for payment of all of your attorney fees, believe your counsel and begin to deal with the possible conflicts of interest discussed above.

Judges' Unstated Critiques of Attorneys

Another explanation for the failure of courts to award comparable fees to the low earner's attorney is that the judge may not consider those fees reasonable in light of the attorney's experience and skill and the complexity of the litigation; that is, the judge may consider the low earner overcharged. Thus, the award is a portion of what the judge believes a reasonable fee to be, not of the actual fee. The process here is a vicious circle. The less attorneys for the low earners can rely on adequate compensation by the court, the more the pool of lawyers available to low earners will be devoid of the most capable practitioners. And as the level of competency is reduced, the courts are even less willing to award comparable compensation.

You should know that judges are not about to reveal in their decisions that they believed one attorney charged excessive fees even if a formal statement of reasons for the decision is requested and is rendered by the court. Judges don't want to embarrass attorneys or make enemies unnecessarily. Judges may also privately harbor the view that the low earner's attorney fees are excessive because part of the work was unnecessary — a commonly held perception among judges. They may feel the attorney has been overly litigious, brought unnecessary motions, or failed to settle the matter in a timely fashion. Thus, the award will be reduced. You will not know of the judge's views. Moreover, some judges consider it irrelevant that the high-earner's attorney has also charged fees in excess of what is reasonable. Judges are likely to feel that what an attorney is paid with one's own money is not subject to court scrutiny beyond the extent to which some misconduct may have caused the other party's attorney fees to be excessive. However, the judge will scrutinize the fees charged by the attorney for the low earner because the court is being asked to make an award of one party's assets to the other.

Finally, some judges shortchange the low earner on a fee award out of a wish not to encourage further litigation in a case the judge believes should settle. (Judges believe *all* cases should settle. There never was a settlement a judge didn't like.) The judge may consider the proceedings up to the point where fees are requested to have been a waste of everyone's time, and may think that if the low earner believes someone else will pay her fees (remember, the low earner is most often the wife), she will file another motion tomorrow and be less willing to settle other issues.

I am not describing a situation where the judge can point to specific conduct by the low earner's attorney that has frustrated the judge's efforts to settle the litigation. As we will discuss later, such conduct is clearly sanctionable under California law by requiring the low earner to pay fees to the other party, or by diminishing the award the low earner might otherwise have received. What I refer to here is just the judge's vague sense that "if I make it profitable for this attorney, the case will take longer than it should."

How Low Earners Can Protect Themselves

Knowing the reluctance of some judges to award the low earner an adequate sum for an attorney, litigants who are low earners can protect themselves to some extent. First, as discussed earlier, certain judges have reputations for inadequate awards, and these judges should be avoided if possible. But in addition, competent attorneys know the fee award increases in direct proportion to the extent the judge perceives that the other party or that party's attorney has created excessive litigation.

The knowledgeable attorney for the low earner will keep a written record of each instance in which the conduct of the opposing attorney or party has caused his or her fees to escalate beyond what is reasonable or expected. A written declaration of this conduct should be presented to the judge during the attorney fee argument and may prove quite helpful if the other attorney has not documented like conduct by you or your attorney.

When *Is a Major Fee Award Issue*

As important as the size of an award is the question of *when* that award is made. The attorney for the low earner does not want to finance litigation by waiting for an award of fees at the settlement conference or trial. California courts have made it clear that the attorney should not have to do so. Attorney fees should be both adequate and, when appropriate, awarded in advance. In theory, the low or nonearning spouse can go into court shortly after an action is filed and obtain an award that will pay his or her attorney fees and costs through trial preparation and up to the settlement conference.

In rather simple litigation, the right to an early award of fees may not be terribly important. The trial may be preceded by a motion or two — perhaps for a restraining order or for support — and then the case is settled. At each motion, the judge can award a modest and reasonable fee to the attorney for the low earner and make a final recommendation on fees at the settlement conference, if necessary.

In a complex case, however, for instance where one party is a self-employed professional or the owner of a business that is entirely or partially community property, an early award of substantial attorney fees to the low earner is critical. Fees for accountants and other experts and for the cost of taking their depositions may exceed $40,000, and the professional or business owner probably will have control over most of the parties' assets that could be used to pay these fees.

Both the low earner's attorney and the experts needed to evaluate the business or professional practice may be unwilling to commence work until a substantial retainer fee is paid. It is unreasonable to expect the attorney for the low earner to advance these fees. An attorney is not expected to finance the litigation and, as explained earlier, a large debt to the attorney can create conflicts of interest over when the home is sold or whether sums paid are to be credited toward spousal support or attorney fees. Indeed, one appellate court has severely chastised a trial judge for refusing to consider an award of fees until the time of trial.[1] But it is interesting to note that this judge was reversed because he was so foolish as to say publicly that it was not his

---

[1] *In re Marriage of Hatch* (1985) 169 C.A.3d 1213.

policy to consider the issue prior to trial. He was not reversed because he refused to make an award.

An adequate award of fees to the low earner is theoretically available early on, and judges are generally more willing to make such awards than they were ten years ago. The only procedural prerequisites of such an award are declarations setting forth the anticipated fees and justifying them in terms of work to be done and hours to be spent. But there is a wide gulf between theory and practice, because attorneys are continually complaining to me that they are not getting adequate fee awards early on when they represent low earners. It is the responsibility of your attorney to know the inclination of the judge who will hear your case.

If a given judge has a preference for deferring an award of fees until after "trial," there is a statute that became effective January 1, 1993, that may be helpful. Family Code Section 2032 allows the judge, in a complex case, to appoint a referee or special master as a case manager to allocate attorney fees and expert fees and provide for payment early on as well as on an ongoing basis. In this way the judge can be assured that an experienced local attorney is overseeing the litigation both for the purpose of seeing that the low earner has adequate funds, but to be sure that funds are awarded only for necessary motions, discovery, and experts. Such an attorney will have an understanding of the value of legal services, and of the importance of an adequate award of fees at the onset of the case. While the special master's rulings are only recommendations to the judge that can be objected to at a hearing set by the aggrieved party, it has been my experience that the recommendations of the case manager are almost never challenged.

Reluctance to Award Advance Fees

There would seem to be two primary reasons for what attorneys claim is a reluctance to award sufficient advance fees: Fear that a substantial award of fees early on will promote litigation, and a desire to see how the litigants and attorneys conduct themselves before awarding fees. These are certainly two thoughts that have run through my mind when asked to award fees early on. These two fears may be directly related to your attorney's reputation with the local judges. If your attorney is known to settle cases reasonably and to refrain from overlitigating cases, the judge may not be as concerned with promoting litigation by making a substantial award of fees.

If your attorney is concerned that the judge does not want to make a substantial award of fees in advance of the litigation because of a desire to first see how the parties have comported themselves in the litigation, your attorney can ask the judge to make an "uncharacterized" award of fees to you. That is, the judge orders the other party to pay you a given sum of money for use in payment of your attorney, but does not then say whether it is the other party's money, community property, or your own funds that are being awarded to you. After the case is concluded, if the judge is satisfied with your and your attorney's conduct in the case, the judge can then rule that the award was the separate property of the other party given to assist you, the low earner. If the judge believes that you have frustrated settlement of the case by your misconduct, the judge can then rule that you received an advance on your share of the community property and the award to you of property at trial will be reduced by the amount of the prior fee award. The judge may want to find that the award came from community property where the judge has made like awards of fees to both parties from a source of liquid community funds.

The concept that the judge will later have an opportunity to mete out rewards and punishments may be illusory in most cases because 95 percent of all cases settle and never go to trial. If the conduct of the other party has greatly increased your attorney fees and made a simple case into a nightmare, even if the case settles on the eve of trial, your attorney can insist on a hearing on attorney fees or, better yet, can condition settlement upon the issue of attorney fees being later submitted to the judge by means of written declarations of both attorneys. As explained earlier, the appointment of a case manager allows the special master who oversees the case management plan to both award fees and monitor conduct at the same time. This may very well be the best way to assure that necessary fees are paid to the attorney for the low earner and that neither party engages in unnecessary litigation.

Another reason for the failure of judges to award fees early on is their inability to identify a source of liquid assets from which payment can be made. But at an early stage in the proceedings, this reason is even more seductive, because the judge can hope that a later sale of assets will result in identifiable funds from which fees can be paid to the low earner. Judges know it is seldom wise to make an order that a party can't comply with. Thus, it appears sensible to defer an order for payment of fees until liquid assets are available. Unfortunately, the employees of the attorney for the low earner do not defer their salaries until the attorney has liquid assets.

If it is obvious that an award of fees cannot be paid immediately, the award can still be made, but payable only when certain property has been sold. If necessary, the court can order interest, which accumulates until payment is made. The truth is that the attorney for the low earner is more apt to stay with the case to completion if an adequate award has been made that needs to be shepherded into his or her purse when assets are sold. To that end, as noted above, a recent change in the law allows you to give your attorney a lien on your interest in community real estate as security for attorney fees. The attorney must advise you in writing to obtain the advice of another attorney before doing so, and you must give the other party notice of your intention and an opportunity to object. Objections that such a lien would make settlement of the case more difficult or force a sale of the home are fairly rare. If objections are filed, then the judge will determine whether the lien may be placed on the property.

There are two tactics used to obtain an award of attorney fees in advance of litigation that your author has seen used by very capable attorneys, and that have proven quite effective.

The first is a tactic for the attorney for the low earner and is often reserved only for judges known to oppose an early award of fees. The attorney files the petition for dissolution or the response in the name of the client, as though the client is a *pro per* (self-represented). Then the attorney files a motion for attorney fees, again in the client's name. By filing in the client's name the attorney is not the attorney of record and thus does not need the court's permission to withdraw from the case. The *pro per* client then appears in court for the hearing on attorney fees. And voila! Who is also present? The attorney! The attorney then tells the judge that the client-to-be, a homemaker during a 30-year marriage and without funds to pay an attorney, has asked said attorney to represent her. The attorney wants to do so, but can only do so if the court will award adequate advance fees to represent the client in a complex case without committing malpractice. The attorney concludes by saying that unless the court provides attorney and expert fees as requested (in a detailed declaration), he or she shall be forced to walk out the courtroom door and leave this poor litigant to fend for herself. This tactic seldom fails, with the exception of once or twice when the judge refused to allow the attorney to make a "special appearance" to ask for fees on behalf of the *pro per* litigant.

It is absolutely necessary that the request for fees be made by the attorney as a "special appearance." If a "general appearance" is made, the attorney cannot withdraw from the case without the judge's permission, and the judge may both refuse to award fees in advance and deny a request to withdraw. If the attorney has to make a general appearance to request fees, the attorney needs to possess a "substitution of attorneys," signed by the client prior to the hearing, that consents to the withdrawal of the attorney. If the client consents, the attorney can withdraw without the judge's permission.

Obviously, the judge doesn't want to be seen as denying someone an attorney. But more important, the judge is faced with the prospect of a lengthy hearing made doubly or triply long because one party is *in pro per*, to say nothing of justifying to the wife and everyone in the courtroom why only one side has counsel. I am personally aware of many cases brought in front of other judges where this tactic has been successful. Nothing makes a judge appreciate lawyers as much as the prospect of a *pro per*. The judge reads the declaration, hears from the other side, and then makes a substantial award of fees. The attorney stays in the courtroom to present other issues, and the judge is spared the bother of a *pro per* litigant.

The second tactic is more insidious, if not devious, and your author is not recommending it to anyone. A few lawyers, when they represent a high earner who has substantial assets and substantial debts, never come to court having taken more than a $500 retainer from their client, Mr. Moneybags. Then, at the hearing early on for attorney fees, they argue, "Judge, the purpose of attorney fees is equality between these parties. You should not put the other attorney in a better position than my client is able to put me." I admit falling for this ruse a time or so before I learned better. The day after the hearing, said attorney will send the client a bill for a $10,000 retainer, which will be paid immediately from liquid assets or borrowed funds. The bill of the low earner's attorney will go unpaid for months if not years.

Thus far, I have discussed attorney fees on an ability/needs basis (the ability of one party to help the other who is in need of assistance) and the tendency of some judges to deny adequate awards out of a desire to limit litigation, award or punish good or bad conduct at a later date when such conduct can be evaluated, or foil overbilling by the attorney for the party seeking the award, among other reasons.

Penalties for Misconduct

The Family Law Act has sections specifically devoted to penalties for misconduct. One section[2] grants the judge the authority to reduce fees to one party or to increase fees awarded against the party with the ability to pay, if that party has frustrated the policy of the court to settle the litigation. Family law is the only area of law with which I am familiar where one can be sanctioned for not settling a case. In all other areas, the litigant is thought to be entitled to a "day in court" as a matter of right.

Another section authorizes the judge to order a party *or an attorney* engaging in frivolous tactics or conduct intended to delay the proceedings to pay attorney fees to the other party.[3]

However, it is important to remember than if an award is made under either section, the party to be sanctioned must be given reasonable notice and a chance to prepare a defense, and the judge must spell out the exact conduct that gave rise to sanctions.

---

[2] Family Code 271(a).
[3] Code of Civil Procedure 128.5.

Who Should Pay the Sanctions

One final word of advice. Every litigant in a family law case is vulnerable to being sanctioned. The sanction, if any, will be a result of a judge's correct or incorrect perception of a situation. But you need to make it clear to your attorney that you will be responsible for any sanctions imposed for your own misconduct, but you will expect your attorney to comply with court rules or to pay sanctions imposed as a result of the attorney's neglect, even though the court may direct you to pay the sanction. This agreement needs to be in writing or at least confirmed by a letter.

This understanding is important because under the section that allows an order for attorney fees as sanctions for frustrating settlement of the case, the judge has no authority to sanction your attorney. You alone can be sanctioned for any misdeeds committed by your attorney. You should readily agree to pay fee sanctions for your conduct — for refusing to authorize settlement, violating court orders, denying visitation, and so forth. But the attorney should pay for sanctions imposed on you for late filing of documents, violations of procedural rules of court, tardiness at a hearing — matters over which you have no control. If you are not present at a hearing or a conference, but are informed by your attorney that you have been sanctioned, you can determine exactly what conduct was sanctioned by calling the judge's clerk or reading a copy of the minutes of the hearing, which are kept by the clerk and are available to you for inspection.

DO'S AND DON'TS

Do...

- Inquire about the judge's reputation for awarding substantial attorney fees early in the litigation.

- Inquire whether an attorney fees hearing is merely *pro forma*, or whether the issues of the award or its amount are still undecided.

- Expect your attorney to ask you to be personally responsible for all fees not paid by your spouse, but determine what collection effort your attorney will make before you are asked for payment.

- Remember that you are paying for educated and informed advice, so when your attorney tells you not to do something because it will not be well received by the judge, listen.

- Make it clear to your attorney that you do not expect to pay sanctions for his or her violations of court rules.

Don't...

- Don't expect your spouse to be ordered to pay all of your attorney fees even if you are unemployed.

- Don't allow attorney fees to be disguised under some other name in the settlement agreement, unless you approve.

- Don't pay your attorney a large retainer before an anticipated early hearing on attorney fees — if your attorney will let you defer part of it. You may wind up being ordered to pay an equal sum to your spouse's attorney.

Summary

If you must be a party to dissolution proceedings, I hope this book will save you substantial money. Although I have made specific suggestions on steps and strategies that may benefit you financially, I will be content if you gain no more than a general understanding of how costly dissolution litigation is apt to be, the legal procedures you may be required to endure, and how judges often decide family law issues. If you now know that a failure to settle your case at an early stage will likely result in a financial disaster for both you and your spouse, that knowledge alone may serve you well. As you face each step in the litigation, you will be more apt to ask your attorney, "What will be the net gain to me if I win?" and "What are my chances of prevailing on this issue?" If the book persuades you to ask these questions, your attorney's work is more likely to be cost-effective.

If you also realize that your choice of an attorney will have an impact on your ability to resolve your disputes with your spouse early on, I suspect you will be more careful in your selection of an attorney and will seriously explore some of the suggested alternative methods for dispute resolution, such as mediation, arbitration, or collaborative law. At a minimum, you are apt to let your attorney know you are aware that a settlement delayed until the settlement conference before a trial (a trial that will probably never take place) is not in your best interest.

Most important, if you take the time and spend the money to hire a competent and capable family law attorney, then by all means take his or her advice. I have never understood why so many people will pay the fees required to hire a first-rate lawyer and then refuse to take the attorney's advice. The majority of attorneys practicing family law are well motivated and view their job to be as much one of peacemaker and settler as that of litigator. If you keep your ego and feelings out of the litigation sufficiently to allow you to approve the compromises the attorney recommends, you will probably be dollars ahead. It is invariably the party who insists on controlling the litigation who overspends in a dissolution case.

Those who wish to criticize this work, whether from financial motivation or a genuine disagreement with my opinions, may well say something to the effect that "his only advice is to settle your case. You don't need a lawyer to do that."

Wrong on both counts. No apology is needed. Indeed, I *am* advising settlement. Those people who settle early almost always do better financially than those who litigate to the bitter end, or even to the settlement conference. I have also sought to tell you how to evaluate a settlement proposal on property, support, and attorney fees.

But most important, you *do* need a lawyer to reasonably settle a case. In family law, trial skills are not nearly as important as negotiation and settlement skills. The attorney who needs to win to meet his or her own ego needs or who uncritically buys into the client's views and emotions is almost worthless in helping you to preserve your estate. In family law, the most valuable assets an attorney has to sell are time and advice in helping you structure a fair and realistic settlement of your case. The attorney who is a mere conduit to the judge of the client's neurotic impulses and demands may very well be rich and successful, but you need not pay for his or her next Mercedes or BMW.

Admittedly, there are cases that cannot be settled because the other side's demands are unreasonable and unchanging. These cases are far less numerous than most people believe, and it is unlikely your case is one of them. But if it is, as you have learned in this book, if you and your attorney can successfully document your spouse's unreasonable posture, he or she will pay a large portion of your attorney fees.

Glossary

abuse of discretion: an order made by a judge that can be said to be so unreasonable that no other judge would make such an order based on the same facts. When judges abuse their discretion, they will be reversed by a Court of Appeals, but courts of appeals seldom find abuse of discretion by the trial judge.

actuary: one who computes what the value or cost of something will be at a later date.

arbitration: the out-of-court resolution of a dispute by the ruling or decision of one who hears evidence and receives facts.

attorney of record: person named by the client as his or her agent and whose name appears on court pleadings and on whom papers can be served.

characterizing: the process by which the judge designates property or money (often attorney fees) as either community or separate property.

charging party: the person bringing the contempt charges. This may either be the other party or the district attorney.

citee: the person charged with contempt.

clinical practice: seeing patients for treatment in a practice, such as psychiatry.

collaborative law: a method for avoiding litigation. The attorneys agree to negotiate to settle the case without bringing motions in court or making formal discovery demands. The parties agree to furnish all information requested by the other party.

community property: property owned jointly by spouses; often acquired by joint effort during the marriage, but can be a gift.

consideration: what one receives in exchange for what one has given.

contingency fee: a charge made by an attorney dependent on a successful outcome in the case; often a percentage of the recovery.

continuance: postponement to a specific date.

costs: filing fees, jury fees, reporter fees at a deposition, etc., as opposed to attorney fees.

credibility: believability.

deed of trust: a type of mortgage.

deposed: questioned under oath (see **deposition**).

deposing: taking a deposition (see **deposition**).

deposition: an oral examination, under oath, by an attorney to determine what the person being deposed will say at trial, or to preserve his or her testimony. The questions and answers are taken down by a court reporter, or may be videotaped. Both attorneys are present, and, occasionally, an expert is present as a consultant for the attorney taking the deposition.

discovery: the process of determining what evidence the other side will present at a hearing or trial. It includes depositions (oral questions and answers recorded under oath), interrogatories (written questions answered in writing under oath), requests for admissions, and requests to produce documents.

dissolution: the legal process by which a marriage is terminated.

divorce-mill attorney: don't hire one.

election motion: a motion insisting that the opposing side make a choice between alternative remedies.

equity: the value of property minus liens or encumbrances.

estate: all that a person owns.

extrinsic fraud: fraud that prevents one from having his or her day in court; it includes failure to give notice of a hearing or providing misinformation that the other party reasonably relies on in court.

family law: relating to law of dissolution, separation, domestic violence, parentage, and child custody jurisdiction; excludes juvenile proceedings.

forensic: characteristic of, or suitable for, a law court; formal argumentation.

good will: reasonable expectation of future business; the reasonable expectation that clients or customers will return or will recommend that their friends do so.

guideline child support: a misnomer for the "presumed correct" figure of child support derived from a statewide algebraic formula that all courts are mandated to follow.

hardship deduction: a deduction from gross income, in addition to taxes, in order to arrive at net disposable income. Child and spousal support are based on the net disposable income of the parties. A hardship deduction for the supporting parent reduces support. A hardship deduction for the supported parent increases support.

heavy hitter: very aggressive attorney known for adversarial skills.

imputed income: income that reflects a party's earning capacity regardless of what he or she may actually earn or not earn.

indefinite spousal support: an award of spousal support that continues "until further order of the court or the death or remarriage of the supported party."

in propria persona (in pro per): without an attorney; unrepresented; self-represented; same as *pro per*.

jurisdiction: authority over a person or property.

lien: a mortgage.

litigant: party to the case; in a divorce case, the spouses are the litigants.

litigation: a lawsuit; contest in a court.

litigious: prone to overuse, or unnecessary use of, the courts to resolve disputes.

malpractice: improper or negligent performance of duties by a professional.

marital property: property normally acquired after marriage; owned by spouses and subject to court distribution at dissolution.

mental health professional: psychiatrist, psychologist, marriage and family counselor, and licensed social worker.

move-away case: see **relocation case.**

net spendable income: income remaining to be spent after all taxes are paid, all expenses allowed as deductions are paid, and child support and spousal support, if any, are deducted from the supporting party's income, and spousal support is added to the supported party's income.

new-mate income: The income of a subsequent spouse or person with whom a party to a support matter is cohabiting at the time of the hearing on support (either child or spousal).

no-fault: the dissolution of a marriage by a judge if one party wishes it dissolved, regardless of who is to blame.

paralegal: a person, not an attorney, with legal skills, who works under direction of an attorney.

pension: retirement benefit.

peremptory challenge: the right to challenge a judge or juror without giving a reason for the challenge. A challenge "for cause" requires that a valid reason be established.

presumed correct figure: The amount of child support required by the statewide guideline (a mathematical formula) after the court has determined the parties' incomes and the amount of time each spends with the children. To vary from the "presumed correct figure," the judge must explain and record how and why the variance is in the best interests of the children.

pro forma: required by procedures but lacking in substance and not needed to accomplish any objective.

pro per: self-represented rather than represented by an attorney in a court action. In some jurisdictions, *pro se* denotes self-representation.

reconciliation: the renewal of marital relations between spouses.

relocation case: a case, often called a move-away case, in which one parent wishes to take the child to another county, state or country. The parent, without the child, is always free to live where he or she wishes.

reservation of jurisdiction: retention by the court of the power to award spousal support at a later date while awarding none at present. If support is not awarded and jurisdiction is not reserved, the court cannot make an award in the future even if the facts then justify it.

retainer fee: amount given to counsel on engaging his or her services and credited against future work to be performed.

sanction: a monetary penalty for violation of court rules or policy.

separate property: the sole property of one spouse, which the court has no jurisdiction to divide or otherwise deal with; opposite of community property.

settler: one who settles.

spousal support: money paid by one spouse to another after separation for support of the recipient; alimony.

stay: to suspend enforcement or action, as in, "The judge stayed the warrant," or "The judge stayed the order."

tax shelter: a transaction that reduces a taxpayer's liability for taxes by providing tax deductions or credits.

testimony: a statement made by a witness under oath.

TRO: a temporary restraining order. This is an order that lasts from the time it is made to the date of the hearing set in the order. It may be granted with or without a hearing, and with or without notice to the other party. TROs can, among other things, award custody, prevent the use or sale of community property, or protect a party against domestic violence. When attorneys refer to TROs without specifying the nature of the TRO they are talking about, they are usually referring to those TROs restraining domestic violence.

vested: an interest, the possession of which at a later date is not contingent upon anything; e.g., a vested right to pension payments is a right that will accrue although the employee may leave the company.

visitation: the right of one parent to visit children of the marriage under order of the court.

wage assignment: a court order served on the employer of the party paying child and/or spousal support that requires the employer to deduct the support from the payor's wages and pay the support directly to the recipient party.

waiver: a relinquishment of a right; "to waive" is to relinquish or give up something.

Index